ADVENTURES OF
HUCKLEBERRY FINN

AN ADAPTED CLASSIC

ADVENTURES OF HUCKLEBERRY FINN

MARK TWAIN

GLOBE FEARON

Pearson Learning Group

Cover designer: Marek Antoniak
Cover illustration: Paul Biniasz

ISBN 0-8359-0224-2
Printed in the United States of America

14 15 16   06 05 04

Globe
Fearon

Pearson Learning Group

1-800-321-3106
www.pearsonlearning.com

ABOUT THE AUTHOR

Mark Twain, whose real name was Samuel Langhorne Clemens, was born in 1835. He spent his youth in Hannibal, Missouri, on the banks of the Mississippi River, the busy highway to America's heartland. As a young man, he piloted steamboats up and down the big river and came to know firsthand the character and raw energy of the expanding nation.

These years on the Mississippi made a lasting impression on Twain's life and works. "In that brief, sharp schooling," he later recalled, "I got personally and familiarly acquainted with about all the different types of human nature." Even his pen name, Mark Twain, came from the signal called out by a steamboatman when the water was deep enough for a safe passage.

Heading west during the Civil War, Twain became a silver prospector in Nevada and a newspaper reporter in California. There he staged a series of public lectures and sent back east his first humorous stories and travel sketches. Twain himself soon moved east to an enthusiastic and growing audience.

Twain was enormously popular throughout his career. He was widely read, appreciated, and honored as few writers ever are. His private life, however, was marked with disappointment. He lost a fortune in failed business schemes and suffered the death of his wife and two of his children. When Twain died in 1910, his fame as a writer, humorist, and lecturer was world wide, but his last years had been bitter and lonely.

Although many of Twain's works are about his boyhood on the Mississippi, he also wrote travel books, detective novels, and stories set in the distant past. His best-known works include *Adventures of Tom Sawyer; Adventures of Huckleberry Finn; Life on the Mississippi; The Prince and the Pauper;* and *A Connecticut Yankee in King Arthur's Court.*

PREFACE

From the time it was published in 1885 until today, Mark Twain's *Adventures of Huckleberry Finn* has remained controversial. Banned in a number of places since it appeared, the book has been censored and argued about for over one hundred years.

The center of the controversy lies in Twain's portrayal of Jim, a runaway slave with whom Huck rafts down the Mississippi. As they begin their journey, Huck treats Jim in the same superior, unfeeling way most whites in Missouri treated black people. Through Huck's colorful and natural language, we see and hear the desperate condition of slaves in the South during the 1800s. Many people object to Twain's realistic descriptions or confuse the author's own attitudes with those of the characters he writes about. They accuse Twain of being racist and crude.

On the other hand, most readers recognize that Twain, through the use of satire and irony, was making fun of the ignorance and hypocrisy of his society. They see Huck's trip down the Mississippi as the story of his own change from a misguided youth to a thoughtful and compassionate person. Huck realizes that slavery is wrong and that even if he "goes to hell" for helping a runaway slave, he is doing the right thing.

Today *Huckleberry Finn* remains as funny, readable, and alive as ever. Students, parents, and educators continue to debate its merits and faults in the classroom and in public. Many editions are in print, and recently Broadway has produced a musical version called *Big River*. Most important, thousands of readers still respond to Twain's rich language, his keen humor, and his deep human sympathy.

Susan G. Bennett, Ph.D.
Associate Professor
Department of Curriculum and Instruction
College of Education
University of Texas at Austin

ADAPTER'S NOTE

This adaptation of *Adventures of Huckleberry Finn* has been made to present the original story in a way that can be more easily understood by the modern reader. To accomplish this goal, a few episodes have been abridged or omitted. In addition, some of the language has been brought up to date.

CONTENTS

1 *I Discover Moses and the Bulrushes.*

If you read that book about Tom Sawyer, you know about me, Huck Finn. The way that book ends is this: We found the money that the robbers hid in the cave, and it made us rich. We got six thousand dollars apiece—all gold. It was an awful sight of money when it was piled up.

Well, Judge Thatcher took it and put it out at interest for us. It brought us a dollar a day apiece, all the year round—more than we could tell what to do with.

Then the Widow Douglas took me for her son, and said she was going to bring me up right. She cried over me, and called me a poor lost lamb, and a lot of other names, too. But she didn't mean any harm by it. She put me in new clothes, and I couldn't do anything but sweat and feel all cramped up. It was tough—living in a house all the time, and everything so regular. The widow rung a bell for supper and you had to come to time. When you got to the table, you couldn't go right to eating. You had to wait for the widow to tuck down her head and grumble a little over her plate—though there wasn't anything the matter with the food.

After supper she got out her book and read to me about Moses and the bulrushes. I was in a sweat to find out all about Moses, till by and by she let it out that he had been dead a long time. Then I didn't care any more about him. I don't take any stock in dead people.

Her sister, Miss Watson, a slim old maid with glasses on, had just come to live there. Now she took a set at me with a spelling book. She worked me hard for about an hour, and then the widow made her ease up. I couldn't have stood it much longer.

Then for an hour it was deadly dull. Miss Watson would say, "Don't put your feet up there, Huckleberry," and "Don't hump up like that, Huckleberry—straighten up." And pretty soon she would say, "Don't gape and stretch like that, Huckleberry—why don't you try to behave?"

Then she told me about the bad place, and I said I wished I was there. She got mad then, but I didn't mean any harm. All I wanted was to go somewhere—all I wanted was a change. She said it was wicked to say that. Said *she* wouldn't say it for the whole world. Said she was going to live so as to go to the good place. Well, I couldn't see anything to gain by going where she was going. I made up my mind not to try for it. But I didn't say so. It would only make trouble and do no good.

She went on and told me all about the good place. She said all a body had to do there was to go around with a harp and sing all day long, forever and forever. I didn't think much of it. I asked her if she thought Tom Sawyer would go there. She said not by a long sight. I was glad about that, because I wanted to be where he was.

Miss Watson kept picking at me, and things got

tiresome and lonesome. Later they brought the slaves in and had prayers. Then everybody was off to bed. I went up to my room with a piece of candle. I set the candle on the table, and then I leaned out the window and tried to think of something cheerful. But it was no use. The stars twinkled away off, and the leaves rustled ever so mournful. After a long time I heard the clock go boom—boom—boom—twelve licks. Then all still again—stiller than ever.

Pretty soon I heard a twig snap down in the dark among the trees. Something was astir. I kept still and listened. Then I could just barely hear a "me-yow! me-yow!" down there. That was good!

"Me-yow me-yow!" I said as soft as I could. I put out the candle and scrambled out of the window onto the shed. Then I slipped down to the ground and crawled in among the trees. And, sure enough, there was Tom Sawyer waiting for me.

2 Our Gang's Bloody Oath

We went tiptoeing along a path, back toward the garden. Right by the kitchen I fell over a root and made a noise. We crouched and kept still.

Miss Watson's big slave, named Jim, was on the kitchen doorstep. We could see him pretty well, because there was a light behind him. He got up and stretched his neck out, listening. Then he said:

"Who dah?"

He listened some more. Then he tiptoed down and stood right by us. We could have touched him, nearly. For minutes and minutes there wasn't a sound, and we all there so close together. A place on my ankle got to itching, but I didn't dare scratch it. Then my ear got to itching, and next my back, right between my shoulders. I thought I'd die if I couldn't scratch. Pretty soon Jim said:

"Say, who is you? Whar is you? Dog my cats if I didn't hear sumf'n. Well, I's goin' to set down here and listen till I hears it again."

He got down on the ground, leaned his back up against a tree, and stretched his legs out. One of them almost touched me. Then my nose got to itching. Soon I was itching in eleven different places. But I didn't dare scratch. I set my teeth hard and tried to stand it. After a while Jim went to breathing hard, and next he was snoring.

Tom made a sign to me and we crawled away on our hands and knees. Pretty soon we stood up and cut along the path around the garden fence. Then we went on, and by and by we fetched up on the top of the steep hill on the other side of town. Here we looked away down into St. Petersburg. We could see three or four lights twinkling, maybe where somebody was sick. And down by the village was the Mississippi River, a whole mile broad, still and grand.

We went down the hill and to the tanyard. There we found Joe Harper and Ben Rogers, and two or three more of the boys, waiting for us. We untied a boat and pulled down the river, two miles, to the big scar on the hillside, and went ashore.

We went to a clump of bushes. Tom stopped there and made everybody swear to keep secret. Then he showed them a hole in the hill, right in the thickest part of the bushes. We lit some candles that Tom had brought, and crawled in on our hands and knees. We went about two hundred yards, and then the cave opened up into a kind of room, all damp and sweaty and cold. There we stopped, and Tom said:

"Now, we will start this band of robbers, and call it Tom Sawyer's Gang. Everybody that wants to join has got to take an oath, and write his name in blood."

Everybody was willing. So Tom got out a sheet of paper that he had the oath on, and read the oath. It swore every boy to stick to the band, and never to tell any of the secrets. And if any person ever did anything to any boy in the band, whichever boy was ordered to kill that person and his family, must do it. And he mustn't eat or sleep till he had killed them and hacked a cross on their breasts, which was the sign of the band. And if anybody in the band told the secrets, he must have his throat cut and have his body burnt up and the ashes scattered all around. And his name would be blotted off the list with blood, and never mentioned again by the gang.

Everybody said it was a beautiful oath. Tom said he got it out of pirate-books and robber-books. He said every gang that was high-toned had that kind of oath.

Some thought we ought to kill the *family* of any boy that told the secrets. Tom said that was a good idea. He took a pencil and wrote it into the oath. Then Ben Rogers said:

"Here's Huck Finn—he hasn't got a family. What you going to do about him?"

"Well, hasn't he got a father?" said Tom Sawyer.

"Yes, but you can't ever find him these days. He used to be always around somewhere drunk. But he hasn't been seen in these parts for a year or more."

They talked it over. I thought I was going to be ruled out. They said that if everybody didn't have a family to kill, it wouldn't be fair and square to the boys that did. I was ready to cry. But all at once I thought of something. I offered them Miss Watson—they could kill her. Everybody said:

"Oh, she'll do. Huck can come in."

"Now," said Ben Rogers, "what is the line of business of this Gang?"

"Nothing, only robbery and murder," Tom said.

"What are we gonna rob?—houses, or cattle, or—"

"Stuff! Stealing cattle is not robbery but burglary," said Tom. "We are not burglars. There's no style to that. We are highwaymen. We stop stages and carriages on the road, with masks on, and kill the people, and take their watches and money."

"Must we always kill the people?"

"Oh, certainly. It will be best to kill them. Except some that we bring to the cave here, and keep till they are ransomed."

"Ransomed? What's that?"

"I don't know, but that's what they do. I've seen it in books."

"But how can we do it, if we don't know what it is?"

"Why, blame it all, we *got* to do it. They all do it. Do you want to go to doing different, and get things all muddled up?"

"Oh, that's all very fine to *say,* Tom Sawyer. But how in the nation are these fellows going to be ransomed if we don't know how to do it to them?"

"Well, I don't know. Maybe it means that we keep them till they are dead."

"Keep them till they are ransomed to death—eating up everything and always trying to get loose!"

"How you talk, Ben Rogers! How can they get loose when we have a guard over them, ready to shoot them down if they move a peg?"

"A guard! So somebody has to stay up all night and never get any sleep, just to watch them. I think that's foolishness. Why can't we take a club and ransom them as soon as they get here?"

"Because that's not the way it's done in the books. Now, Ben Rogers, do you want to do things in the regular way or not?"

"Oh, all right, I don't mind. Say, do we kill the women too?"

"Kill the women? No; nobody ever saw anything in the books like that. You bring them to the cave, as polite as pie. And by and by they fall in love with you, and never want to go home any more."

"Mighty soon the cave will be so cluttered up with women, and fellows waiting to be ransomed, there won't be any room for the robbers. But go ahead, have it your own way."

Little Tommy Barnes was asleep now. When they waked him up he was scared, and cried. He said

he wanted to go home to his ma, and didn't want to be a robber. They all made fun of him, and called him a cry-baby. That made him mad, and he said he would go straight and tell all the secrets. Tom paid him five cents to keep quiet. Then Tom said we would all go home and meet next week, and rob somebody and kill some people.

Ben Rogers said he wanted to begin next Sunday. He said Sunday was the only day he would be free. But all the boys said it would be wicked to rob and kill on Sunday, and that settled that. They agreed to get together and fix a day as soon as they could. They elected Tom Sawyer first captain, and Joe Harper second captain, of the Gang. Then we started home.

I climbed up the shed and crept into my window just before daybreak. I had got my new clothes all dirty with clay, and I was dog tired.

3 We Ambush the Arabs

I got a good going over in the morning, from old Miss Watson, on account of my clothes. But the widow didn't scold. She just cleaned off the clay and looked so sorry that I thought I would behave a while, if I could.

Then Miss Watson took me into the closet and prayed. She told me to pray every day, and whatever I asked for I would get. I tried it. Once I got a fishline, but no hooks. The line wasn't any good without hooks. I tried for the hooks three or four times, but couldn't make it work. One day I asked Miss Watson to try for me, but she said I was a fool.

I went out into the woods and had a long think about it. I said to myself: If people can get anything they pray for, why can't Deacon Winn get back the money he lost on pork? Why can't the widow get back her silver snuff-box that somebody took? Why can't Miss Watson fat up? I went and asked the widow about it. She said all that people could get by praying was "spiritual gifts." This was too much for me, so she explained what "spiritual gifts" meant. It meant that I must help other people and look out for *them* all the time, and never think about myself.

I went out into the woods and turned that over in my mind a long time. I couldn't see any good in it—except for the other people. So I reckoned I wouldn't worry about it, just let it go.

Sometimes the widow would talk to me about Providence in a way to make a body's mouth water. But maybe next day Miss Watson would take hold and knock it all down again. I judged there must be two Providences. A poor chap would stand a good chance with the widow's Providence, but if Miss Watson's Providence got him, there was no more help for him. I reckoned I would belong to the widow's Providence, if she wanted me. But I couldn't see how her Providence was to be any better off for having me, seeing I was so ignorant and so kind of lowdown and ornery.

Well, we played robber now and then about a month, and then I quit. All the boys did. We hadn't robbed anybody, never killed any people, but only just pretended. I couldn't see any profit in it. We used to hop out to the woods and go charging down on hog drivers and women in carts taking garden stuff to market. And one time Tom sent a boy to run about town with a blazing stick, which was the sign for the Gang to get together. He said he had got secret news by his spies that a whole band of Spanish merchants and rich A-rabs would be camped next day in Cave Hollow. They had two hundred elephants and six hundred camels and over a thousand pack-mules, all loaded with diamonds. They had a guard of only four hundred soldiers. He said we must slick up our swords and guns and get ready. He would never go after even a turnip cart, but he must have the swords and guns all scoured up for it.

I didn't believe we could lick such a crowd of Spaniards and A-rabs. But I wanted to see the camels and elephants, so I was on hand next day, Saturday.

We all hid near where the camels and elephants would pass. When we got the word, we rushed out of the woods and down the hill. But I didn't see any camels or elephants, nor even any Spaniards or Arabs. It was nothing but a Sunday School picnic, and only a primer class at that.

We busted it up, and chased the children up the hollow. We got some doughnuts and jam. Ben Rogers picked up a rag doll, and Joe Harper got a song book. Then the teacher charged in, and made us drop everything and run.

I didn't see any diamonds, and I told Tom Sawyer so. He said there were loads of them there—and Arabs and elephants, too. I said why couldn't we see them, then? He said magicians had turned the whole thing into an infant Sunday School, just to spite us. I said:

"Then the thing for us to do now is to go after the magicians."

"Huck Finn, you are a numskull. Why, a magician would call up a lot of genies, and they would hash you up before you could say Jack Robinson. They are as tall as a tree and as big around as a church."

"Well," I said, "suppose we got some genies to help us. Couldn't we lick the other crowd then?"

"How are you going to get them?"

"I don't know. How did *they* get them?"

"They rub an old tin lamp or an iron ring. Then the genies come tearing in, with thunder and lightning ripping around and smoke rolling everywhere. Then they do everything you tell them to do. They think nothing of pulling up a shot-tower by the roots, and belting a Sunday School superintendent over the head with it."

"Who makes them tear around so?"

"Why, they belong to whoever rubs the lamp or the ring. They have got to do whatever he says. Maybe build a palace forty miles long out of diamonds, and fill it full of chewing gum. Maybe fetch an emperor's daughter from China for you to marry. And they have got to do it before sun-up next morning, too. And more: they have got to waltz that palace around over the country, wherever you want it."

I said, "I think they are a pack of flatheads for not keeping the palace themselves. And what is more—I'd see a man in Jericho before I'd drop my business and come to him, for the rubbing of an old tin lamp."

"Why, you'd *have* to come when he rubbed it, whether you wanted to or not."

"What! and I as high as a tree and as big as a church! All right, then; I *would* come. But I'd make that man climb the highest tree in the country when I got there."

"Shucks, Huck Finn. You don't seem to know anything—a perfect saphead."

I thought all this over for two or three days. Then I decided I would see if there was anything in it. I got an old tin lamp and an iron ring. I went out in the woods and rubbed till I sweated like an Injun, thinking to build a palace and sell it. But it was no use. None of the genies would come.

4 Pap Comes Back

Pap hadn't been seen for more than a year, and that was all right with me. I didn't ever want to see him again. He always whaled me when he was sober and could get his hands on me. I used to take to the woods when he was around.

One day a body was found in the river, drowned, about twelve miles above St. Petersburg. People said the body was just Pap's size, had long hair, and wore ragged clothes. They thought it was Pap, though they couldn't tell by the face, because it had been in the water so long it wasn't much like a face at all. But I wasn't so sure. I thought the old man would turn up again by and by, but I wished he wouldn't.

Three or four months went along. It was well into the winter now. I had been to school most of the time. I had learned to spell and read and write a little. I could say the multiplication table up to six times seven is thirty-five. At first I hated the school, but by and by I got so I could stand it. Whenever I got too tired of it I played hookey. The hiding I got next day was good for me, and cheered me up. So the longer I went to school, the easier it got to be for me.

One morning there was an inch of snow on the ground. Down by the garden I saw some tracks.

Somebody had stood around there a while, and then gone on around the garden fence. I didn't need anybody to tell me who had made the tracks.

That night when I lit my candle and went up to my room, there was Pap, tilted back in a chair, quite at home. I used to be scared of him all the time, he tanned me so much. But now, after the first jolt, I wasn't scared worth bothering about.

His hair was long and greasy, and hung down over his eyes like vines. His face, where it showed above his black whiskers, was white—a tree-toad white, a fishbelly white. As for his clothes—just rags. He had one ankle resting on the other knee. The shoe on that foot was busted, and two of his toes stuck through. His hat was on the floor—an old black slouch with the top caved in.

I stood looking at him; he kept still, his chair tilted back a little. I set the candle down. I noticed the window was up; so he had climbed in by the shed roof. He kept looking me all over. By and by he said:

"Starchy clothes—very. You think you are a good deal of a big-bug, *don't* you?"

"Maybe I am, maybe I'm not," I said.

"Don't give me none of your lip. I'll take you down a peg before I get done with you. You are educated, too, they say—can read and write. Who told you you might meddle with such hifalutin' foolishness, hey?—who told you you could?"

"The widow. She told me."

"The widow, hey? Well, I'll show her how to meddle. And looky here—you drop that school. You hear? Bringing up a boy to put on airs over his own father. None of your family could read and write. *I* can't. And here you go swelling yourself up like this. I ain't

the man to stand it—you hear? Say, lemme hear you read."

I took up a book and started to read. When I had read about half a minute, he gave the book a whack with his hand and knocked it across the room.

"It was so," he said; "you can do it. Now looky here; you stop that putting on frills. I'll lay for you, my smarty, and if I catch you about that school, I'll tan you good."

He kept on mumbling and growling a minute, and then he said:

"*Ain't* you a sweet-scented dandy, though? A bed, and bed-clothes, and a lookin'-glass, and a piece of carpet on the floor. And your own father got to sleep in the tanyard. I'll take some of the frills out of you before I'm done with you. They say you are rich. Hey?—how about that?"

"They lie—that's how."

"Looky here—I am a-standin' about all I can—so don't gimme no sass. I have been in town two days, and I ain't heard nothing but about you bein' rich. I heard about it away down the river, too. That's why I'm here. You get me that money tomorrow—I want it. Say, how much you got in your pocket?"

"I got only a dollar, and I want that to—"

"Makes no difference what you want it for—you just shell it out."

He took it and said he was going down town to get some whiskey. When he was out the window on the shed roof, he put his head in again and cussed me for putting on frills. He said he'd lay for me and lick me, if I didn't drop that school.

Next day he was drunk. He went to Judge Thatcher and tried to make him give up the six thousand dollars, but the judge wouldn't. Then Pap went for Judge Thatcher in court, to make him give up that money. Pap went for me, too, for not stopping school. He caught me a couple of times and thrashed me. But I went to school just the same. I dodged him or outran him most of the time. I hadn't wanted to go to school before, but I went now to spite him.

Then Judge Thatcher and the Widow Douglas went to court to get the law to make one of them my guardian. But the case was brought before a new judge that had just come to town, and he didn't know Pap. He said courts mustn't interfere and separate families if they could help it—said he would rather not take a child away from its father.

That pleased Pap. He caught me and said he would cowhide me till I was black and blue if I didn't raise some money for him. I borrowed three dollars from Judge Thatcher. Pap took it and got drunk again, and went blowing around cussing and whooping and carrying on all over town, until about midnight. Then they jailed him again for a week. But he said *he* was satisfied, said he was boss of his son, and was going to make it warm for *him*.

When Pap got out of jail, the new judge said he was going to make a man of him. He took Pap into his own house, dressed him up clean, and had him to breakfast, dinner and supper, with the family. After supper the judge talked to Pap about stopping his drinking. Pap cried and said he had been a fool and had fooled away his life. Now he was going to turn over a new leaf. He would be a man that nobody would be ashamed of. He said he had always been misunderstood, that what a man wanted when he was down and out, was sympathy.

The judge said he believed him, and the judge's wife cried over Pap. Then the old man signed a pledge—made his mark. They tucked him into a beautiful room, the spare room.

In the night he got powerful thirsty, and climbed out on the porch roof, and slid down to the ground. He went and traded his new coat for a jug of whiskey, and then climbed back up into the bedroom. Toward daylight he crawled out again, drunk as a fiddler, and rolled off the porch to the ground. He broke his left arm in two places and almost froze to death before somebody found him after sun-up.

The judge said maybe a body could reform the old man with a shotgun, but he didn't really know any other way.

5 *I Fool Pap and Get Away*

That law trial was a slow business. So every now and then I would borrow two or three dollars from Judge Thatcher and give it to Pap, to keep from getting a thrashing. Every time I let him have money he got drunk. And every time he got drunk, he raised cain around town and got jailed. This just suited him fine.

He kept hanging around the widow's house, where I lived, until she told him if he didn't stay away she would make trouble for him. Well, wasn't he mad! He said he'd show who was Huck Finn's boss. So he watched out for me one day in the spring, and caught me, and took me up the river, about three miles, in a boat. We crossed over to the Illinois shore, where there was an old log hut in a place where the timber was so thick you couldn't find it if you didn't know where it was.

We lived in that old cabin and fished and hunted for a living. Every few days he locked me in, and went to the store at the ferry, three miles below. At the store he traded fish and game for whiskey, and then got drunk and licked me.

The widow found out where I was, by and by, and she sent a man over to try to get hold of me. But Pap drove him off with a gun.

Two months or more went along. I got used to the place, and liked it—all but the thrashing part. It was kind of lazy and jolly to fish and hunt all day, no books nor study. I didn't have to wash and comb up. Nor go to bed and get up regular. Nor eat on a plate and have old Miss Watson pecking at me all the time. I got so I didn't want to go back. It was pretty good times in the woods.

But by and by Pap got too handy with his hickory. I was all over welts. He got to going away so much, too, and leaving me locked in. Once he locked me in and was gone three days. I was scared. I made up my mind I would fix up some way to leave there.

There wasn't a window big enough for a dog to get through. The door was thick, solid oak slabs. I found an old rusty wood-saw stuck in between a rafter and the roof. One day when Pap was away, I greased it and got it ready for use. An old horse-blanket was nailed against the logs at the far end of the cabin, behind the table. This was to keep the wind from blowing through the chinks and putting the candle out. I got under the table and raised the blanket, and went to work to saw a hole through the big bottom log. It was a good long job, but I was getting toward the end of it when I heard Pap's gun in the woods. I dropped the blanket and hid my saw. Pretty soon Pap opened the door.

He wasn't in a good humor—so he was his natural self. He said he had been down town and everything there was going wrong. His lawyer had said he could win the lawsuit and get the money, if they ever got started on the trial. But Judge Thatcher would know how to keep putting it off. And he said people thought there'd be another trial to get me away from Pap and give me to the widow, and they guessed it would win this time. This news shook me up. I didn't want to go back to the widow's and live so "sivilized," as they called it.

Then the old man got to cussing. He cussed everybody he could think of, and then cussed them all over again to make sure he hadn't skipped any. He said he'd like to see the widow get me. He said there was a place six or seven miles off that he could stow me in, and they might hunt till they dropped and they couldn't find me.

That made me pretty uneasy again. I wouldn't stay on hand till he got that chance.

The old man made me go to the skiff* and bring in the things he had brought. There was a fifty-pound sack of corn meal, and a side of bacon, ammunition, and a four-gallon jug of whiskey. I toted all the things up to the cabin. The old man took a swig or two and went to ripping again. Whenever his liquor had begun to work he always went for the government. This time he says:

"Call this a gov'ment! Here's the law a-standin' ready to take a man's son away from him. Yes, just as I have got him raised and ready to go to work for me, and give me a rest. The law takes a man like me—worth six thousand dollars, and jams him into an old cabin like this—and lets him go round in clothes not fit for a hog. They call that gov'ment! Sometimes I've a mighty notion to leave the country for good and all. Yes, and I told old Thatcher so to his face. Lots of people heard me. I said, 'For two cents I would leave the blamed country and never come a-near it again.'

"Oh, yes, this is a wonderful gov'ment, wonderful. Why, looky here. There was a free Negro there

---

* A light boat.

from Ohio, almost as white as a white man. And there ain't a man in that town that has got as fine clothes as he had—a gold watch and chain, and a silver-headed cane. And what do you think? They said he was a professor in a college, and could talk all kinds of languages. And that ain't the worst. They said he could *vote* when he was at home. Right then I says, 'I'll never vote again!' They all heard me. And the country may rot for all me—I'll never vote again as long as I live—"

Pap was going on so, he never noticed where his old limber legs took him. So he went head over heels over the tub of salt pork, and barked both his shins. The rest of his speech was the hottest kind of language. He hopped around the cabin, first on one leg and then on the other, holding first one shin and then the other. Then he let out with his left foot all of a sudden and gives the tub a rattling kick. But that was the boot that had a couple of his toes leaking out the front end of it. He raised a howl, and down he went and rolled there and held his toes. And the cussing was hotter than any he had ever done before.

"Well, don't stand there all day," Pap said. "Out with you and see if you find any fish on the lines. I'll be along in a minute."

I cleared out up the river bank. I noticed some tree limbs floating down and a sprinkling of bark. The river was beginning to come up. I could have a great time now over at the town. With the June rise, cordwood would come floating down, and pieces of log rafts—sometimes a dozen logs together. All you had to do was to catch them and sell them to the wood-yards and the saw mills.

I went along up the bank, with one eye out for Pap and the other out for what the river might bring

along. Well, all at once here comes a canoe, a beauty, about fifteen feet long, riding high like a duck. I shot head first off the bank like a frog, and struck out for the canoe.

I climbed in and paddled her ashore. I'd just hide her, and when I was ready to run away, instead of taking to the woods, I would go down the river. I rowed her into a little creek all hung over with vines and willows, and left her there.

Pretty soon Pap comes out, and we go along the bank, looking at the river. It was coming up pretty fast, with lots of driftwood going down. By and by along comes part of a log raft—nine logs fast together. We went out with the skiff and towed it ashore. Right away he must shove right over to St. Petersburg and sell. So he locked me in, and took the boat, and started off, towing the raft.

Then I out with my saw and went to work on that log again. Before he was on the other side of the river, I was out of the hole. I took some corn meal and bacon and coffee and sugar, and put it in the canoe. Then I took two blankets, the skillet and the coffee-pot. I took fish-lines and matches and candles, and other things—everything that was worth a cent. I cleaned out the place. I wore the ground a good deal, crawling through and dragging out so many things. But I scattered dust over the ground and put the piece of log back in its place. If you stood a few feet away, you wouldn't even notice a thing.

It was all grass clear to the canoe, so I hadn't left a track. Then I got the gun and went up a piece into the woods and shot a wild pig. I took this fellow back to the cabin and smashed the door in with the ax. Then I took the pig inside, hacked into his throat with the ax, and laid him down to bleed.

Well, next I took an old sack and put a lot of big rocks in it—all I could drag—and started it from the pig and dragged it down to the river. You could see plain enough that something had been dragged over the ground. I dumped it in the river, and down it went out of sight.

Last I pulled out some of my hair, stuck it on the bloody ax, and slung the ax into a corner. Then I took up the pig and held him so he wouldn't drip till I got a good piece below the house, and then dumped him in.

"All right," I thought, "now they will think my dead body is in the river. I can stop anywhere. Jackson's Island is good enough for me. I know that island pretty well, and nobody ever goes there. Then I can paddle over to town nights, and slink around and pick up things I want. Jackson's Island is the place."

I went to the canoe. It was night now, but the moon was so bright I could count the drift logs that went slipping along, black and still. The river looked miles and miles across.

I went spinning down the stream in the shade of the bank, for about two miles. Then I struck out toward the middle of the river. Pretty soon I would be passing the ferry landing, and people might see me and hail me. I could hear people talking at the ferry landing; then the talk got further and further off, as I went on below the ferry. About two miles down stream, there was Jackson's Island, standing in the middle of the river, big and dark and solid.

It didn't take me long to get there. I shot past the head at a ripping rate, the current was so swift. Then I got into the dead water and landed on the side toward the Illinois shore. I parted the willows and pushed the canoe into a deep dent in the bank. Then I landed and made fast the canoe.

First I went up to the head of the island and looked out on the big river. Three or four lights winked over in St. Petersburg, two or three miles away. Then I went into the woods and stretched out for a nap before breakfast.

6 *I Spare Miss Watson's Jim*

The sun was up high when I waked, but I just stayed there in the grass and the cool shade, feeling lazy and rested. A couple of squirrels on a limb jabbered at me very friendly.

I was dozing off again when I heard a deep sound of "Boom!" away up the river. I roused up and rested on my elbow to listen. Pretty soon I heard it again. I hopped up and went and looked out at a hole in the leaves. A bunch of smoke was resting on the water a long way up—about abreast of the ferry. And there was the ferry boat, full of people. "Boom!" The white smoke squirted out of the ferry boat's side. Then I understood what was the matter. They fired a cannon over the water to make my dead body come to the top.

I was pretty hungry, but it wouldn't do to start a fire. They might see the smoke. So I stayed there and watched the cannon smoke, and listened to the boom. The river was a mile wide, and it always looked pretty on a summer morning. I was having a good time seeing them hunt for my body, if only I had a bite to eat. The ferry boat was floating with the current. By and by she drifted in so close to the island I could see everybody on the boat, Pap and Judge Thatcher and Joe Harper and Tom Sawyer and his Aunt Polly and his brother Sid, and plenty more.

Everybody was talking about the murder. The captain spoke up:

"Look sharp now. The current sets in the closest here. Maybe he has washed ashore and got tangled among the brush at the water's edge. I hope so."

I didn't hope so. They all crowded up and leaned over the rails, nearly in my face. I could see them, but they couldn't see me. The boat floated on, and went out of sight around the island. I could hear the booming now and then, farther and farther off.

Now I was all right. Nobody would come hunting after me. I got my traps out of the canoe and set up camp in the thick woods. I made a kind of tent out of my blankets, to put my things under, so the rain couldn't get at them. I caught a catfish and haggled him open with my saw, and toward sunset I started my campfire and had supper. Then I set out a line to catch some fish for breakfast. When it was

dark I stayed by my campfire, feeling pretty well
satisfied. But by and by I got sort of lonesome. So I
went out to the bank and listened to the water wash-
ing along, and counted the drift logs coming down.
Then I went to bed.

And so for three days and nights. No difference—
just the same thing. But the next day I went exploring
through the island. I was boss of it; it all belonged
to me, so to speak, and I wanted to know all about
it. I found plenty of strawberries, ripe and good—
and green grapes and green raspberries and black-
berries. They would come in handy by and by, I
judged.

Well, I went fooling along in the deep woods,
till I wasn't far from the foot of the island. I had
my gun but I hadn't shot anything. About this time
I nearly stepped on a good-sized snake. It went sliding off through the grass and flowers, and I after

it, trying to get a shot at it. All of a sudden, I bounded right into the ashes of a campfire, still smoking.

My heart jumped up amongst my lungs. I went sneaking back on my tiptoes as fast as ever I could. Every now and then I stopped among the thick leaves and listened, but my breath was coming so hard I couldn't hear anything else. If I saw a stump, I took it for a man. If I trod on a stick and broke it, my breath was cut in two, and I only got half, and the short half, too.

When I got to camp, I wasn't feeling very brash. There wasn't much sand in my craw. I got all my traps into my canoe again, and put out the fire, and scattered the ashes around to look like an old last-year's camp. Then I climbed a tree. I was up in the tree about two hours. But I didn't see anything, didn't hear anything. I only *thought* I heard and saw a thousand things. Well, I couldn't stay up there forever. So at last I got down, but I kept in the thick of the woods, and on the lookout all the time.

I had nothing to eat but what was left over from breakfast, and some berries. By the time it was night I was pretty hungry. So when it was good and dark I slid out from the shore before moonrise and paddled over to the Illinois bank. There I went out in the woods and cooked a supper. I made up my mind I would stay there all night. Then I heard a *plunkety-plunk, plunkety-plunk.* I said to myself, horses coming. Next I heard people's voices.

I got everything into the canoe as quick as I could, shoved out and paddled away. I tied up on the island, in the old place, and slept in the canoe. I didn't sleep much. Everytime I waked up I thought somebody had me by the neck. After a while I saw a pale streak over the treetops. Day was coming. I said to myself I can't live this way; I will find out who is on this island with me or bust. Well, I felt better right off.

Pretty soon it was light, and I took my gun and slipped off toward where I had run across that campfire, stopping every minute or two to listen. By and by, sure enough, I caught a glimpse of a fire, away among the trees. I went for it cautious and slow. When I was close enough to have a look, I saw a man on the ground. He had a blanket around his head, and his head was nearly in the fire. I got behind a clump of bushes, in about six feet of him, and kept my eyes on him. Pretty soon he stretched himself and hove off the blanket. It was Miss Watson's Jim! I bet I was glad to see him.

"Hello, Jim!" I said, and skipped out from behind the bushes.

He bounced up and stared at me wild. Then he dropped down on his knees and put his hands together and says:

"Don't hurt me—don't! I ain't never done no harm to a ghost. I always liked dead people, and done all I could for 'em. You go and git in de river again whah you belongs."

I wasn't long making him understand I wasn't dead. I was ever so glad to see Jim. I wasn't lonesome now. I told him I wasn't afraid of *him* telling the people where I was. I talked along, but he just looked at me, never said a thing. Then I said:

"Let's get breakfast. Make up your campfire."

"What is de use makin' up de campfire to cook strawberries and such truck?"

"Strawberries and such truck!" I said. "Is that what you live on? How long you been on the island, Jim?"

"I come heah de night after you was killed. I'm so hungry I could eat a hoss. But you got a gun. Now you kill sumf'n, and I'll make up de fire."

We went over to where the canoe was. While he built a fire in a grassy open place amongst the trees I fetched the bacon and coffee-pot and frying-pan, and sugar and tin cups. When breakfast was ready we lolled on the grass to eat it, smoking hot. Jim laid it in with all his might, for he was about starved. By and by I said:

"How do you come to be here, Jim; and how'd you get here?"

He looked pretty uneasy and didn't say anything for a minute. Then he said:

"You wouldn't tell on me if I was to tell you, would you, Huck?"

"Blamed if I would, Jim."

"Well, I—I *run off!* But mind, you said you wouldn't tell."

"I said I wouldn't, and I'll stick to it. So now, tell me all about it."

"Well, you see, Miss Watson—she always say she wouldn't sell me down to Orleans. But I notice a slave trader round de place lately, and I begin to get uneasy. Den one night I hear Miss Watson tell de Widder Douglas dat she was about to sell me down to Orleans. She said she'd get eight hundred dollars for me, and she couldn't give up such a big stack of money. I lit out mighty quick. I tuck out up de river road. I'd made up my mind about what to do. You see, if I tried to get away afoot, de dogs 'ud track me. If I stole a skiff, dey'd miss dat skiff and know about whah to pick up my tracks on de yuther side. So a raft is what I's after. By and by I see a lantern light coming down de river. So I wade in and shove a log ahead and swim out in de river. When de raft come along I tuck a-hold de back end. De men was all in de middle whah de lantern was. So I climb up. I reckoned by early daylight. I would be twenty-five miles down de river. Den I would swim ashore and take to de woods on de Illinois side. But poorty soon a man starts to come back wid de lantern. So I slid overboard and struck out fer dis island. And here I is, nearly starved."

Some birds flew along, going a yard or two at a time, and then lighting. Jim said that was a sign it was going to rain. Jim could tell all kinds of signs. He said if you count things you are going to cook for dinner, you'll have bad luck. And you'll have bad luck if you shake the table cloth after sundown. Jim said if a man owns a beehive and that man dies, the bees must be told about it before sun-up next morning. Else the bees will all quit work and die.

I asked him if he could tell me any good luck signs. He said:

"Mighty few—and dey ain't no use to a body. Why you want to know when good luck is comin'? Want to keep it off? But I know one good luck sign—if you got hairy arms and breast, it's a sign dat you is goin' to be rich."

"Have you got hairy arms and breast, Jim?"

"What's de use to ax dat question? Don't you see I has?"

"Well, are you rich?"

"No, but dat won't prove de sign is no good. You see, maybe you is got to be po' a long time fust. Yes; and I's rich now, come to look at it. I owns myself, and I's worth eight hundred dollars. I wisht I had de money, I wouldn't want no mo'."

7 The House of Death Floats By

I wanted to go and look at a place near the middle of the island that I had found when I was exploring. So we started, and soon got to it. The island was only three miles long and a quarter of a mile wide.

The place was a long, steep ridge about forty feet high. We tramped and climbed around all over it, and by and by we found a good big cave in the rock, up near the top. Jim was for putting our traps in there right away. So we went back and got the canoe and paddled up abreast of the cave. Then we lugged all the traps up there.

The door of the cave was wide, and on one side of the door, the floor stuck out a little. We built a fire there and cooked dinner. We spread the blankets inside for a carpet to eat our dinner on. Pretty soon it darkened up and began to thunder and lighten. It was one of these regular summer storms. It looked all blue black outside and lovely, and the rain thrashed along so thick the trees off a little way looked dim. And then a perfect ripper of a gust would bend the trees down and turn up the pale underside of the leaves. Now and then the lightning would flash as bright as glory, and the thunder would let go with an awful crash and then go rumbling and tumbling down the sky.

"Jim, this is nice," I said. "I wouldn't want to be anywhere else but here. Pass me along another hunk of fish and some hot cornbread."

The river went on rising and rising, for ten or twelve days. At last it was over the banks. The water was three or four feet deep in the low places on the island. Daytimes we paddled all over the island in the canoe. We went winding in and out among the trees. In some places the vines hung so thick we had to back out and go some other way. On every old broken-down tree you could see rabbits and snakes and such things. And in a day or two they got so tame, on account of being hungry, that you could paddle right up and put your hand on them—but not the snakes and turtles—they would slide off into the water. The ridge our cave was on was full of them. We could have had pets enough, if we had wanted them.

One evening late—we didn't show ourselves in broad daylight—we caught a little section of a lumber-raft, made of nice pine planks. It was twelve foot wide and about fifteen foot long, and floated above water about six or seven inches—a solid level floor. We tied it up to the shore.

Another time here comes a frame-house floating down, tilted away over. We paddled out and got aboard—climbed into a room through a window. There was a bed in there, and a table, and two old chairs, and lots of things scattered about on the floor—old greasy cards and whiskey bottles. Everything was so scattered and tumbled about, we judged the people had left in a hurry. There was something on the floor over in the far corner, that looked like a man. So Jim said:

"Hello you!"

But it didn't move. So I hollered again, and then Jim said:

"De man ain't asleep. You stay here—Lemme go see."

He went, and bent down, and looked. "It *is* a dead man. Been shot in de back. Dead two or three days maybe. Keep away—he looks too awful."

I didn't look. Jim piled some old rags on the body, but I wouldn't have looked anyway. Two old dirty calico dresses hung against the wall, and a sun-bonnet, and some men's clothing, too. We found eight dollars in silver, sewed up in the lining of an old overcoat. We found an old tin lantern, and a lot of tallow candles, and a tin cup, and an old bed quilt, and a hatchet, and some nails, and a dog collar, and a horseshoe. Just as I was leaving I found a pretty good curry comb, and Jim found an old fiddle bow, and a wooden leg. The wooden leg was too long for me and not long enough for him, and we couldn't find the other one, though we hunted all around. We put all of it into the canoe—it might come in handy.

Well, the days went along, and the river went down between its banks again. One morning I said I would slip over the river and find out what was going on. Jim said I must go in the dark and look sharp. Then he said couldn't I dress up like a girl?

So we shortened up one of the calico dresses, and I turned my trouser-legs to my knees and got into it. I put on the sun-bonnet and tied it under my chin. Jim said nobody would know me, even in the daytime.

I started to the shore in the canoe just after dark, and the drift of the current fetched me in a little below the town. I tied up and started along the bank. A light was burning in a little shanty that hadn't

been lived in for a long time. I slipped up and peeped in at the window. There was a woman about forty years old in there, knitting by a candle. She was a stranger to me. But if she had been in that little town two days, she could tell me all I wanted to know.

I knocked at the door, and made up my mind I wouldn't forget I was a girl.

8 *They Are After Us!*

"Come in," said the woman, and I did. "Take a chair."

I did. She looked me all over with her little shiny eyes, and said, "What might your name be?"

"Sarah Williams. I live in Hookerville, seven miles below. I've walked all the way and I'm all tired out."

"Hungry, too, I reckon. I'll find you something to eat."

"No, I'm not hungry. I stopped two miles below here at a farm. My mother is down sick, and out of money. She sent me to tell my Uncle Abner Moore. He lives at the upper end of the town. Do you know him?"

"No, but I don't know everybody yet. I haven't lived here quite two weeks. It's quite a way to the upper end of the town. You better stay here all night. Take off your bonnet."

"No," I said, "I'll rest a while, and go on. I'm not afraid of the dark."

She said she wouldn't let me go by myself. Her husband would be in by and by, and she would send him along with me. Then she got to talking about her husband—and about her relations up the river— and about her relations down the river—and about how much better off they used to be—and how they had made a mistake coming to this town, instead of letting well enough alone—and so on and so on.

I was afraid *I* had made a mistake coming to her to find out what was going on in the town. But by and by she got around to Pap and the murder. Then I was pretty willing to let her clatter along.

She told about me and Tom Sawyer finding the twelve thousand dollars (only she got it twenty)— and all about Pap, and what a hard lot he was—and what a hard lot I was. At last she got down to where I was murdered.

I said, "We heard about it down in Hookerville. But we don't know who it was that killed Huck Finn."

"At first everybody thought old Finn had killed him. But before night, they judged it was done by a runaway slave named Jim. He run off the very night Huck Finn was killed. So there's a reward out for him—three hundred dollars. And there's a reward out for old Finn too—two hundred dollars. You see, old Finn went boo-hooing to Judge Thatcher to get money to hunt for the murderer. The judge let him have some, and old Finn got drunk and went off with a couple of mighty hard-looking strangers. Well, he hasn't come back, and people think now that he killed his boy to get Huck's money. People say he wasn't any too good to do it."

I was so uneasy I couldn't keep still. I had to do something with my hands. I took up a needle off the table and went to threading it. My hand shook and I made a bad job of it.

"But you can't prove anything on old Finn, you know. If he stays away for a year, everything will be quieted down then, and he'll walk right into Huck's money."

"Has everybody quit thinking the runaway slave killed him?"

"Oh, no, a good many think he did. They'll get him pretty soon now, and maybe they can scare the truth out of him. I don't think he's far from here— but I'm not talking it around. I've seen smoke over on Jackson's Island. So I think that slave is hiding over there. My husband is going over to see. He and another man went up town to get a boat and borrow another gun. They'll go over tonight. Three hundred dollars is a lot of money to pick up."

The woman kept looking at me, and I didn't feel a bit easy. Pretty soon she said:

"What did you say your name was, honey?"

"M-Mary Williams."

"Honey, I thought you said it was Sarah."

"Oh, yes, I did. Sarah Mary Williams. Sarah is my first name. Some call me Sarah, some call me Mary."

"Oh, that is the way of it?"

"Yes." I was feeling better, but I couldn't look up yet. Then the woman fell to talking about the rats being as free as if they owned the place. She was right. You would see one stick his nose out of a hole in the corner every little while. She said she had to have things handy to throw at them. She handed me a bar of lead twisted up into a knot, and told me to try for one. Well, the next time a rat showed his nose, I let drive. If he had stayed where he was, he'd have been a mighty sick rat.

She said that was first-rate, and I would get the next one. She went and got the bar of lead. "You better have this in your lap, handy," she said. She dropped the bar into my lap, and I clapped my legs together to catch it.

Then she looked me straight in the face, very
pleasant and said: "Come, now, what is your real
name? Is it Bill, or Tom, or Bob—or what is it?"

I shook like a leaf. I didn't know what to do, but

I said, "Please don't poke fun at a poor girl like me. If I'm in the way here, I'll—"

"Stay where you are. Bless you, child, I wouldn't tell on you. You must trust me, and I'll help you. So will my old man, if you want him to. You've run away from somebody that treated you bad. Tell me all about it now, like a good boy."

So I said I would just make a clean breast and tell her everything. I told her I was an orphan, and the law had bound me out to a mean old farmer, thirty miles back from the river. He treated me so bad I stole some of his daughter's clothes and cleared out. I was going to my Uncle Abner Moore.

"Hold on a minute. I'll put you up a snack to eat. You might want it."

So she put me up a snack, and said: "Say, when a cow is down on the ground, which end of her gets up first? Answer up now—don't stop to study over it. Which end gets up first?"

"The hind end."

"Well, then, a horse?"

"The forward end, mum."

"Which side of a tree does the moss grow on?"

"North side."

"When fifteen cows browse on a hillside, how many of them eat with their heads pointed in the same direction?"

"The whole fifteen, mum."

"Well, I reckon you *have* lived in the country. I thought you might be trying to hocus me again. What is your real name, now?"

"George Peters, mum."

"Well, try to remember it, George. And don't go around women in that old calico dress. You might fool men, maybe, but not women. And bless you, child, when you set out to thread a needle, don't hold the thread still and bring the needle up to the thread. Hold the needle still and poke the thread at it. That is the way a woman does it, but a man always does it the other way. And when you throw at a rat or anything, fetch your hand up over your head and throw stiff-armed from the shoulder, like a girl, and miss your rat by six or seven feet. Don't throw from the wrist and elbow with your arm out to one side, like a boy. And, mind you, when a girl tries to catch anything in her lap, she throws her knees apart. So don't clap your knees together the way you did when you caught the lump of lead. Why, I spotted you for a boy when you threaded the needle, and I tried the other things on you just to make certain. Now trot along to your uncle, Sarah Mary Williams George Peters. And if you get into trouble send word to Mrs. Judith Loftus, which is me, and I will do what I can to get you out."

I slipped back to where my canoe was, a good piece below the house. I jumped in and was off in a hurry. I landed and slopped through the timber and up the ridge and into the cave. There Jim was, sound asleep on the ground.

"Get up and hump yourself, Jim! There's not a minute to lose. They are after us!"

Jim asked no questions, he didn't say a word. But the way he worked for the next half hour showed how he was scared. By that time everything we had in the world was on our raft. I paddled the canoe out from the shore a little piece, and took a look around. If there was a boat anywhere about, I couldn't see it. Then we got out the raft and slipped along down the banks, past the foot of the island, keeping dead still, never saying a word.

$\mathcal{9}$ Honest Loot from the Fields

It must have been after midnight when we got below the island at last. The raft seemed to go mighty slow. We planned, if we saw a boat coming after us, to take the canoe and break for the Illinois shore. It was well a boat didn't come. We hadn't thought to put the gun in the canoe, or a fishing line, or anything to eat. We had been in too much of a sweat to think of so many things. It wasn't good judgment to put *everything* on the raft.

When the first streak of day showed, we tied to a towhead on the Illinois side. A towhead is a sandbar with cottonwoods on it as thick as harrow teeth. We hacked off some branches with the hatchet, and covered up the raft with them. We stayed there all day. The channel at that place was down the Missouri shore. We watched the rafts and steamboats spin down the Missouri shore and the up-bound steamboats fight the big river in the middle.

That evening, when it was beginning to come on dark, we poked our heads out of the cottonwood thicket, and looked up and down and across. Nothing in sight. So Jim took up some of the top planks of the raft and built a snug wigwam to get under when the weather was blazing hot or rainy. Right in the middle of the floor of the wigwam we put a layer of dirt about five or six inches deep, with a frame around it to hold the dirt in place. This was to build a fire on, in sloppy or chilly weather.

We made an extra steering oar, too. One of the others might get broken or lost. We fixed up a short forked stick to hang the old lantern on. We must always show a light when a steamboat was coming, to keep from being run over.

That night we floated between seven and eight hours, with a current that was making over four miles an hour. We caught fish and talked, and took a swim now and then to keep off sleepiness. It was kind of solemn, drifting down the big still river, looking up at the stars. We didn't talk loud, and when we laughed it was only a low chuckle.

We traveled during the night and hid in the daytime. We had mighty good weather, and nothing happened that night, nor the next, nor the next. Every night we passed towns, some of them away up on black hillsides, nothing but just a shiny bed of lights. One night we passed St. Louis, and it was like the whole world lit up.

As soon as daylight showed, we stopped and tied up. Then we cut young cottonwoods and willows and hid the raft, and set out the fishing lines. Next we slid into the river and had a swim, to freshen up and cool off. Then we rested on the sandy bottom where the water was about knee-deep, and watched the daylight come. Not a sound anywhere—the whole world asleep—only maybe sometimes the bullfrogs a-cluttering.

Soon as it was night, out we shoved. When we got the raft out to about the middle of the river we let her float wherever the current wanted her to. Then we dangled our legs in the water, and talked about all kinds of things. We stayed naked, day and night, whenever the mosquitoes would let us. It was lovely, living on a raft. We had the sky up there, all speckled with stars. We would look up at them and talk about whether they had been made or only just happened. Jim said he thought they had been made. I said they had happened—it would take too long to *make* so many. Jim said the moon could have *laid* them. That looked reasonable. I have seen a frog lay almost as many, so it could be done. We liked to see falling stars come streaking down. Jim said maybe they had got spoiled and had to be hove out of the nest.

Every now and then I would slip ashore toward ten o'clock, at some little village, and buy ten or fifteen cents worth of meal or bacon or other stuff. Sometimes I lifted a chicken that wasn't roosting comfortable, and took him along. Pap always said, "Take a chicken when you get a chance, because if you don't want him yourself, you can find somebody that does." But I never saw Pap when he didn't want the chicken himself.

Mornings before daylight, I slipped into corn fields and borrowed a watermelon, or some new corn, or things of that kind. Pap always said it was no harm to borrow things if you meant to pay them back sometime. But the widow said it was a soft name for stealing, and no decent body would do it. Jim said he reckoned the widow was partly right and Pap was partly right. The best way would be for us to pick out two or three things and say we wouldn't borrow them anymore. We tried to make up our minds whether to stop borrowing watermelons or cantaloupes or mushmelons, or what. We decided to stop borrowing crabapples and persimmons. I was glad we got it settled this way. Crabapples never are very good, and persimmons wouldn't be ripe for two or three months yet.

We shot a water-fowl now and then, that got up too early in the morning or didn't go to bed early enough in the evening. Take it all round, we lived pretty high.

One night we had a big storm after midnight, with a power of thunder and lightning. The rain poured down in a solid sheet. We stayed in the wigwam and let the raft take care of itself. When the lightning glared out, we could see a big straight river ahead and high rocky bluffs on both sides. By and by I said:

"Jim, looky yonder!"

It was a steamboat that had killed herself on a rock. The lightning showed her very plain. She was leaning over, with part of her upper deck poking up above water.

"Let's land on her, Jim."

But Jim was dead against it at first. "I don't want to go foolin' round no wreck."

"We might borrow something worth having out of the captain's stateroom. Cigars, I bet you—and cost five cents apiece. Stick a candle in your pocket. I can't rest, Jim, till we give her a going over. Tom Sawyer would never go by this wreck. He'd go aboard it if it was his last act. And wouldn't he throw style into it—wouldn't he spread himself. Why, you'd think he was Christopher Columbus discovering Kingdom Come!"

Jim grumbled, and then agreed to go. The lightning showed us the wreck again, just in time. We went up to it, and made fast.

10 Honest Loot from the Walter Scott

We sneaked aboard, feeling the way with our feet and spreading our hands out before us. Pretty soon, by jiminy, away down through the hall we saw a light. In the same second we heard low voices.

Jim whispered that he was feeling sick, and for me to come away. Just then I heard a voice wail out:

"Oh, please don't, boys, I swear I won't ever tell!"

Another voice spoke, pretty loud: "You always want more than your share. And you always got it, too; because you promised if you didn't you'd tell. But this time you have said it one time too many. You are the meanest hound in this country."

In a minute Jim was gone for the raft. But I said to myself, "Tom Sawyer wouldn't back out now, and I won't either." So I dropped on my hands and knees, and crept along until I saw a man stretched on the floor, and two men standing over him. One of them had a dim lantern in his hand. The other one had a pistol pointed at the man's head on the floor. He was saying:

"I'd like to! And I ought to—a mean skunk!"

The man on the floor would shrivel up and say, "Oh, please don't, Bill. I won't ever tell!"

" 'Deed you *won't!* You never said a truer thing than that. Hear him beg! And yet if we hadn't got the best of him and tied him up, he'd have killed us both."

52

"Put up that pistol, Bill," said the man with the lantern. "I don't *want* him killed, and I have my reasons for it."

"Bless your heart, Jake Packard!" said the man on the floor, sort of blubbering. "I'll never forget you long as I live!"

Packard didn't take any notice of that. He hung up his lantern on a nail, and motioned Bill to follow him. They started toward where I was, there in the dark. I crawfished as fast as I could, and crawled into a stateroom. I heard the men coming, pawing along through the dark.

"Here—come in here," said Packard.

And in they stepped. But before they got in I was in the upper berth, cornered, and sorry I had come. They stood there with their hands on the edge of the berth and talked, low and earnest. Bill wanted to kill the man.

"He has said he'll tell, and he will—he'll turn state's evidence. I say put him out of his troubles."

"So do I," said Packard, very quiet.

"Well, then, let's go and do it."

"Hold on a minute. You listen to me. It won't be more than two hours before this wreck breaks up and washes off down the river. See? He will be drowned and nobody to blame for it but himself. That way is just as good, and brings no risk of a halter for us."

"All right, then. Come along."

So they left and I crawled out of there all in a cold sweat. It was dark as pitch out on deck. I said in a coarse whisper, "Jim." He answered up, right at my elbow, with a sort of moan.

"Quick, Jim, there's a gang of murderers in yonder. We must hunt up their boat and set her drifting down the river. Then the sheriff can get all of them. Quick—hurry! I'll hunt this side, you hunt that. Start at the raft, and—"

"Oh, my lordy, lordy! Dey ain't no raft. She done broke loose and gone!"

I caught my breath and almost fainted. Shut up on a wreck with such a gang of murderers! We had to find their boat now—had to have it for ourselves. So we went quaking and shaking along until we got to the stern. No sign of a boat. Jim said he couldn't go any farther, he was so scared he had no strength left. But I said:

"Come on. If we get left on this wreck, we are in a fix, sure."

So on we prowled again. When we got pretty close to the cross-hall door, there was their skiff! In another second I'd have been aboard her, but just then the door opened. One of the men stuck his head

out only a couple of feet from me. He flung a bag
of something into the boat, and then got in himself.
It was Packard. Then Bill walked out and got in.
Packard said in a low voice:

"All ready—shove off!"

"Hold on," Bill said. "Did you search him?"

"No. Didn't you?"

"No. So he has his share of the cash yet. Come
along—no use to take truck and leave money."

So they got out and went back inside. In half a
second I was in the boat, and Jim tumbled in after
me. I out with my knife and cut the rope, and away
we went!

We didn't touch an oar, and we didn't speak nor
whisper. We went gliding along, dead silent, past
the wreck. In a minute or two more the boat was a
hundred yards below the wreck, and darkness soaked
her up.

Then Jim manned the oars, and we took out after our raft. Now I was worried about the men. I thought how dreadful it was, even for murderers, to be in such a fix. No telling, I might come to be a murderer myself yet, and then how would I like it? So I said to Jim:

"The first light we see, we'll land a hundred yards above or below, and find a good hiding place for you and the boat. I'll go find somebody to get that gang out of their scrape. Then they can be hung when their time comes."

Pretty soon it began to storm again. The rain poured down. We boomed along down the river, watching for lights and for our raft. By and by a lightning flash showed us a black thing floating ahead, and we made for it.

It was the raft, and we got aboard again, mighty glad. Then we saw a light on shore, away down to the right. So I said I'd go for it in the skiff. I told Jim to float along on the raft, and keep a light burning, till I got back. The skiff was half full of plunder that the gang had taken from the wreck. We hustled it on the raft in a pile. Then I took the skiff and shoved for the light. As I got down towards it, three or four more lights showed—up on a hillside. It was a village. The shore light was a lantern on a ferry boat. I skimmed around and found the watchman asleep. I shook his shoulder two or three times, and then began to cry. He stirred up in a kind of startled way, and said:

"Don't cry, bub—oh, dang it now, *don't* take on so. What's the trouble?"

"Are you the watchman of this boat?"

"Yes, and I'm the captain, and the owner, and the mate, and the pilot, and head deck-hand. And sometimes I'm the freight and passengers. I'm not as rich as old Jim Hornback, but I wouldn't trade places with him—"

I broke in. "Miss Hooker is in an awful peck of trouble. If you would take your ferry boat and get her off the wreck—"

"You mean the *Walter Scott?*"

"Yes."

"Why, great goodness, she had better get off mighty quick. How in the nation did she ever get on that wreck?"

"She was visiting up there at that town—you know—"

"Yes, I know—Booth's Landing—go on."

"She was visiting at Booth's Landing, and just at night we started to cross the river. She was going to stay all night at a friend's house, Miss What-you-may-call-her—I don't remember her name. Well, we lost the steering oar, and went floating down till we hit on the wreck. I was the only one that could swim, so I made a dash for it. Miss Hooker said if I didn't find help sooner, to come here and hunt up her uncle. Now if you'll go and—"

"By Jackson, I'd *like* to, but who's going to pay for it?"

"Why, *that* will be all right. Miss Hooker told me that her Uncle Hornback—"

"Great guns! is *he* her uncle? Looky here. You break for that light over yonder, and tell Jim Hornback I've gone to get his niece. Hump yourself, now. I'm going around the corner to rouse out my engineer."

As soon as he turned the corner I pulled up shore and tucked myself in among some wood-boats. I waited to see the ferry boat start. But before that happened, here comes the wreck, dim and dusky, sliding along! A cold shiver went through me. I struck out for her.

She was floating very deep, not much chance of anybody being alive in her. I pulled all around her and hollered, but nobody answered. All dead still.

Then here comes the ferry boat. So I shoved toward the middle of the river till I was out of eye-reach. Then I stopped and looked back to see the ferry boat go and smell around the wreck. But pretty soon the captain saw no hope of anybody being alive on the wreck, and he went for shore.

I laid into my work and went a-booming down the river. I felt a little heavy-hearted about the gang, but not much. If they could stand it, I could.

It seemed a long time before Jim's light showed up. When it did show, it looked a thousand miles off. By the time I got there the sky was beginning to get a little gray in the east. We struck for an island, hid the raft, and turned in and slept like dead people.

11 *Was Solomon Wise?*

When we got up, we turned over the truck that the gang had taken off the wreck. We found boots, and blankets, and clothes, and a lot of books, and a spy glass—all sorts of things. We had never been so rich before in our lives. We spent all that afternoon in the woods talking and having a good time. I told Jim all about what had happened inside the wreck. I said that that was "adventure." Jim said he didn't want any more adventure. He said when he found the raft gone, he judged it was all up with him. He might get drowned. He might get saved, but whoever saved him would send him back home to get the reward, and then Miss Watson would sell him South sure. Well, he was right. He generally was right; he had an uncommon level head.

I read to Jim about kings and dukes and earls, and how they called each other "your majesty" and "your grace" and "your lordship," instead of mister. Jim's eyes bugged out, he was so interested.

"I didn't know dey was so many of 'em," he said. "I ain't heard much about none, 'cept dat old King Solomon, and dem kings in a pack of cards. How much pay do a king get?"

"Why they can get a thousand dollars a month— they can have just as much as they want. Everything belongs to them."

"Ain't dat gay? And what have dey got to do, Huck?"

"Why, nothing! How you do talk! They just lazy around."

"Is dat so?"

"Of course it is. They just lazy around—except maybe when they go to war. Other times when things get dull and don't go to suit them, they whack some heads off. But mostly they hang round the harem."

"Round de which?"

"Harem."

"What's de harem?"

"The place where he keeps his wives. Don't you know about the harem? Solomon had one; he had about a million wives."

"A harem is a boardin' house, I reckon. Most likely dey has rackety times in de nussery. And de wives quarreling all de time and addin' to de noise. Dey say Solomon was de wisest man dat ever lived. I don't take no stock in dat. Would a wise man want to live in such a racket all de time? No—'deed he wouldn't. A wise man would build a boiler factory. He could shut *dat* down when he want to rest."

"Well, but he *was* the wisest man. The widow told me so herself. Why, once when two women went to him to decide which was the mother of a child they both claimed, you know what Solomon said?"

"No, what he say?"

"He said, 'Chop the child in two and each of you take half.'"

"And did dey do it?"

"No, one woman said she didn't want half a child—said the other woman could have it all."

"Well, dat is de beatenest notion in de world! You just take a look at dat a minute. Suppose I's Solomon.

You is one of de women and dat stump dah is de yuther woman. Dis here dollar bill is de child. You both claims it. What does I do? Does I shin round among de neighbors to find out who de bill *do* belong to and hand it over to de right one, like anybody with gumption would do? No; I whacks de bill in *two,* and gives half to you and half to her. Now what use is half a bill?—can't buy nothin' with it. And what use is half a child? I wouldn't give a dern for a million of 'em."

"But hang it, Jim, you miss the point!"

"Don't talk to me about your points. I reckon I knows sense when I sees it, and dey ain't no sense in any such doings as dat. De quarrel wasn't about a half child; it was about a whole child. De man dat tries to settle a quarrel about a whole child by offering half a child—he don't know enough to come in out of de rain. Don't talk to me about Solomon bein' a wise man."

"But I tell you, you don't get the point."

"Yes, I gets de point—I gets de *real* point. De real point is down deeper. It lays in de way Solomon lived. A man with only one or two children ain't goin' to be wasteful of 'em. He can't afford it. But a man with about five million children running round de house is different. He would as soon chop a child in two as a cat. A child or two more or less wasn't nothin' to Solomon, dad fetch him!"

If Jim got a notion in his head once, there was no getting it out again. So I went on talking about other kings, and let Solomon slide. I told him about Louis Sixteen that got his head cut off in France, long time ago. And about his little boy, the dolphin,*

* Huck's misspelling of "dauphin," title of the eldest son of kings of France.

that they took and shut up in jail. "But some say he got out and came to America."

"But dey ain't no kings here, is dey, Huck?"

"No."

"Den he can't get no job. What he goin' to do?"

"Well, I don't know. Some of them get on the police force, and some teach people how to talk French."

"Why, Huck, don't de French talk de same way we does?"

"No, Jim. You couldn't understand a word they said—not a single word. Suppose a man comes up to you and says *Polly-voo-franzay*—what would you think?"

"I wouldn't think nuffin'. I'd take and bust him over de head, if he wasn't white. I wouldn't let him call me dat."

"Shucks, that's the Frenchman's way of saying, 'Do you know how to talk French?' "

"And a blame silly way. Ain't no sense in it."

"Looky here, Jim. Does a cat talk the same way we do?"

"No."

"Well, does a cow?"

"No."

"And it's natural and right for a cat and a cow to talk different from *us*?"

"Course."

"Then why can't it be natural and right for a Frenchman to talk different from us? You answer me that."

"Is a cat a man, Huck?"

"No."

"Is a cow a man?"

"No."

"Well, den, dey ain't no sense in dem talkin' like a man. Is a Frenchman a man?"

"Yes."

"*Well,* den! Dad blame it, why don't he *talk* like a man? You answer me *dat!*"

I see it warn't no use wasting words. . . . So I quit.

12 *Fooling Poor Old Jim*

We judged we were getting close to Cairo, where the Ohio River comes in. There we would sell the raft, and get on a steamboat, and go away up the Ohio, amongst the free states. Then Jim would be out of trouble.

Well, the next night a fog began to come on. We made for a towhead to tie to, for it wouldn't do to run in a fog. I paddled ahead in the canoe, with the line of the raft, meaning to make fast. But there wasn't anything but little saplings to tie to. I passed the line around one, growing on the edge of the bank. There was a stiff current, and the raft boomed down so lively she tore the sapling out by the roots, and away she went.

It made me so sick and scared I couldn't budge for half a minute. By then there was no raft in sight—you couldn't see twenty yards in the fog. I jumped into the canoe and grabbed the paddle, but she didn't move. I hadn't untied her.

As soon as I got started, I took out after the raft hot and heavy. But the minute I was out in the solid white fog, I hadn't any more idea where I was going than a dead man.

I had to let the boat drift in the current. It wouldn't do to paddle—I would run into a bank or something. I whooped and listened. Away down somewhere I heard a whoop, and I went tearing after it. The next time I heard it, I was heading away to the right of it. And the next time, I was heading away to the left of it. I did wish the fool would think to beat a tin pan, and beat it all the time, but he never did. Well, I fought along, and directly I heard the whoop *behind* me.

The whooping went on, and in about a minute I went booming down on to a bank with smoky ghosts of big trees on it. The current swung me off to the left, and I shot among a lot of snags, where the water fairly roared, it was tearing by them so fast.

In another second or two I was past these, and the fog was solid white again. I couldn't hear a sound. I kept still, listening to my heart thump. I didn't draw a breath till it thumped a hundred. Now I understood. That bank was an island, and Jim had gone down on the other side of it. It was no sand bar that you could float by in ten minutes. It had the big timber of a regular island. It might be five or six miles long.

If you think it is not lonesome out in a fog, all by yourself in the night, you try it once—you'll see. You float along, of course, four or five miles an hour, but you *feel* that you are dead still on the water. If a glimpse of a snag slips by, you don't think how fast *you* are going. You think, my! how that snag is tearing along.

For about half an hour I whooped every now and then. At last I heard the answer, a long way off. I tried to follow it, but I got into a nest of islands. I had dim glimpses of them on both sides—sometimes just a narrow channel between. I had to claw away from the bank pretty lively four or five times to keep from knocking an island out of the river. I judged Jim's raft must be butting into a bank every now and then—it was floating along a little faster than I was.

By and by I seemed to be in the open river again. But I didn't hear a sign of a whoop anywhere. The raft had run on a snag maybe, and it was all up with Jim. I was so tired I stretched out in the canoe. I couldn't bother any more. I would take just one little cat-nap.

When I waked up, the sky was full of bright stars. The fog was all gone, and I was spinning down a big bend. I looked down stream, and saw a black

speck on the water, I took after it, but when I got near, I saw it was just a couple of saw logs made fast together. Then I saw another black speck and chased that, then another, and this time I was right. It was the raft.

When I got to it, Jim was asleep, with his head down between his knees, and his right arm hanging over the steering oar. The other oar was smashed off, and the raft was littered with leaves and branches. She had had a rough time, too.

I tied the canoe to the raft, and went and stretched out right under Jim's nose, as if I had been asleep there.

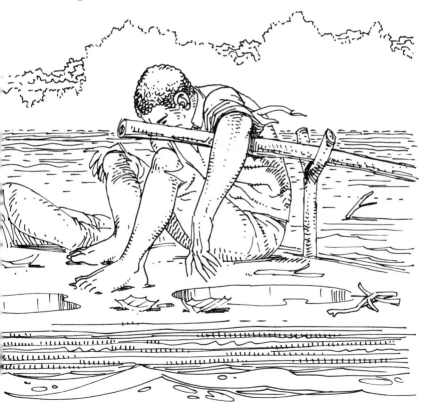

"Hello, Jim. Have I been asleep? Why didn't you stir me up?"

"Goodness gracious, is dat you, Huck! You ain't drowned—you is back again! Honey, it is too good for true. Lemme look at you, chile. Lemme feel of you. You is back again—de same old Huck, thanks to goodness!"

"Why, what makes you talk so wild? Why do you talk about my coming back, as if I had been gone away?"

"Huck—Huck Finn, you look me in de eye. *Hain't* you been gone away?"

"Gone away? Where would I go to?"

"Well, sumf'n is wrong. Is I heah or whah *is* I? Now dat's what I wants to know."

"You are here plain enough. But I think you are a tangle-headed old fool, Jim."

"I is, is I? Well, you answer me dis: Didn't you tote out de line in de canoe fer to make fast to de shore?"

"No I didn't. What shore?"

"Looky here. Didn't de line pull loose and let de raft go a-hummin' down de river and leave you in de canoe in de fog?"

"What fog?"

"De fog dat is been around all night. Didn't you whoop and didn't I whoop till we got mixed up in de islands? Didn't I bust up against a lot of dem islands and 'most get drowned?"

"Well, this is too many for me, Jim. I have seen no fog, nor islands. I was here talking with you all night, till we both went to sleep. You have been dreaming."

"But, Huck, it's all just as plain to me as—"

"Makes no difference how plain it is. There's

nothing in it. I know, because I have been here all the time."

Jim studied over it for five minutes, then said:

"Well, I reckon I did dream it, Huck. But dog my cats if it wasn't the plainest dream I ever had."

"Tell me all about the dream, Jim."

Jim went to work and told me the whole thing right through, just as it happened, though he painted it up some. Then he said he must 'terpret the dream, because it was sent for a warning. He said the towhead stood for a man that would try to do us some good. But the current was another man that would get us away from him. The whooping was warnings that would come to us. The nest of islands was troubles we would get into with all kinds of mean folks. Then I said:

"What do *these* things stand for?" I pointed to the leaves and rubbish on the raft.

Jim looked at the trash, and looked at me, and back at the trash again. Then he looked at me steady without smiling, and said:

"When I went to sleep here, my heart was most broke, because you was lost. I didn't care no mo' what become of me and de raft. When I woke up and find you back, all safe and sound, I could have got down and kissed yo' foot, I was so thankful. And all you was thinkin' about was how you could make a fool of old Jim wid a lie. Trash is what people is dat puts dirt on de heads of friends and makes 'em ashamed."

Then he got up and went into the wigwam. I felt mean, but it was fifteen minutes before I could go and humble myself to him. But I did, and I wasn't ever sorry for it afterward. I didn't do him any more mean tricks. I wouldn't have done that one, if I'd thought it would make him feel that way.

13 *We Look for Cairo*

We went drifting down into a big bend. The night clouded up and got hot. The river was very wide, and walled with timber on both sides. We couldn't see a break in it, hardly ever, or a light. We talked about Cairo and wondered whether we would know it when we got to it. I said likely we wouldn't unless the houses happened to be lighted up. Jim said if the Ohio River and the Mississippi River joined together there, that would show.

There was nothing to do now but look out sharp for the town, and not pass it without seeing it. Jim said he'd be mighty sure to see it, because he'd be a free man the minute he saw it, but if he missed it he'd be in a slave country again. Every little while he would jump up and say, "Dah she is!"

But it was only lightning bugs. Jim said it made him all over trembly to be so close to freedom. Well, it made me all over trembly too, to hear him. I had begun to get it through my head that he *was* almost free. And who was to blame for it? Why, *me*. I couldn't get that out of my conscience. It got to troubling me so I couldn't stay still in one place.

I tried to make out to myself that *I* wasn't to blame—I didn't run Jim off from his rightful owner.

But it was no use. Conscience would up and say:

"But you could have paddled ashore and told somebody he was running for his freedom."

That was so—and that was where it pinched. Conscience would say:

"What did poor Miss Watson ever do to you that you could see her slave go right off under your eyes, and never say a word? What did that poor old woman do to you that you could treat her so mean? Why, she tried to get you to learn your book and your manners. She tried to be good to you, *that's* what."

Every time Jim danced around and said, "Dah is Cairo!" it went through me like a shot. And if I thought it *was* Cairo, I'd nearly die of misery.

Jim talked out loud all the time I was talking to myself. When he got to a free state, he said, he was going to save up money to buy his wife. Then they would both work to buy their two children. If their master wouldn't sell them, he would get somebody to go and steal them.

It almost froze me to hear such talk. Here was this slave, who I had helped to run away, coming right out flat-footed and saying he would steal his children—children that belonged to a man I didn't even know—a man that hadn't ever done me any harm. My conscience got to stirring me up hotter than ever. At last I said to it:

"Let up on me—it's not too late yet—I'll paddle ashore at the first light and tell."

Then I felt easy, all my troubles gone. By and by a light showed up. Jim sings out:

"Dat is de good old Cairo at last; I just knows it! We is safe, Huck! Jump up and crack yo' heels!"

"I'll take the canoe and go and see, Jim. It might not be, you know."

He jumped and got the canoe ready. As I shoved off he said:

"Soon I'll be a-shoutin' for joy. I'll be a free man. And I couldn't ever been free if it hadn't been for Huck. You is de best friend Jim ever had. And you is de *only* friend old Jim has got now."

I paddled off, all in a sweat to tell on him. When I was some yards off he called:

"Dah you goes, de old true Huck."

Well, I just felt sick. But I said to myself, "I *got* to do it—I can't get *out* of it."

Then along comes a skiff with two men in it with guns. They stopped and one of them said:

"Do you belong on that raft yonder?"

"Yes, sir."

"Any men on it?"

"Only one, sir."

"Well, five slaves have run off tonight, up above the bend yonder. Is your man white or black?"

I tried to answer right up, but the words wouldn't come. I wasn't man enough to come out with the truth. I hadn't the spunk of a rabbit. I felt myself weakening, so I just quit trying, and said:

"He is white."

"I reckon we will go and see for ourselves. Come, boy, buckle to your paddle, and let's get along."

I bent to my paddle and they bent to their oars. When we had made a stroke or two, I said:

"Pap will be mighty glad. He's sick. Maybe you'll help me tow the raft ashore. I can't do it by myself. Everybody goes away when I ask them to help."

"Well, that is mighty mean. Odd, too. Say, boy, what is the matter with your father?"

"Well, I'll be honest—but don't leave us, please. He has the—"

They backed water. "Keep away, boy! He has the smallpox, and you know it. Do you want to spread it all over?"

"Well," I said, blubbering, "I told everybody before, and they went away and left us."

"We are right down sorry for you, but—well, hang it—we don't want the smallpox. Look here, I'll tell you what to do. You float along down about twenty miles. You'll come to a town on the left-hand side of the river. When you ask for help, tell them your father is down with chills and fever. Don't be a fool again and let people guess what is the matter. Now, we are trying to do you a kindness. So you just put twenty miles between us. It won't do you any good to land yonder where the light is. Nothing there but a wood-yard. Here, I'll put a twenty-dollar gold piece on this board. You get it when it floats by. I feel mighty mean to leave you. But, my kingdom, it won't do to fool with smallpox."

"Hold on, Parker," said the other man. "Here is a twenty to put on the board for me. Good-bye, boy."

They went off and I went back to the raft, feeling pretty low. I had done wrong, but I wouldn't be feeling any better if I had told the truth and caused Jim to be caught. What was the right thing to do? I was stuck.

We talked about the money. It was a pretty good raise—twenty dollars apiece. Jim said we could take deck passage on a steamboat now, and the money would last us as far as we wanted to go in the free states.

Toward daybreak we tied up. Jim worked all day fixing things in bundles and getting ready to quit rafting.

That night about ten we hove in sight of the

lights of a town away down on the left-hand bend. I went off in the canoe to ask about it. Pretty soon I found a man out in the river with a skiff, setting a trot-line. I paddled up and said:

"Mister, is that town Cairo?"

"Cairo, no. You must be a blame fool."

"What town is it, mister?"

"If you want to know, go and find out. If you stay here bothering around me for about half a minute longer, you will get something you don't want."

I paddled to the raft. Jim was awful disappointed. But I said never mind, Cairo would be the next place, maybe.

We passed another town before daylight, and I was going out again. But we saw the bank was high ground, so I didn't go. No high ground about Cairo, Jim said. We tied up for the day to the left-hand bank. I said:

"Maybe we went by Cairo in the fog that night."

"Don't talk about it, Huck."

When it was broad daylight, here was the clear Ohio water inshore, and outside was the regular old Muddy! So we *had* passed Cairo.

We couldn't take the raft up the stream, of course. The only thing was to wait for dark and go back in the canoe. So we slept all day among the cotton-wood thickets. When we went back to the raft about dark, the canoe was gone!

We didn't say a word for a good while. By and by we talked it over. There wasn't a thing to do but go along down the river with the raft, till we got a chance to buy a canoe to go back up the river in. So we shoved out after dark on the raft. The place to buy canoes is off rafts tied up at shore. But we didn't see any rafts tied up. So we went along three hours or more. The night got gray and thick, which is the next meanest thing to fog. You can't see any distance.

Then along comes a steamboat up the river. We lit the lantern and judged she would see it. We could hear her pounding along, but didn't see her till she was close, and she was aimed right for us. She was a high one, and coming in a hurry, looking like a black cloud with rows of glow-worms around it. All of a sudden she bulged out, big and scary, with a long row of wide-open furnace doors shining like red-hot teeth, and her great bows and guards hanging right over us.

There was a yell at us and a jingling of bells to stop the engines, a powwow of cussing, and whistling steam—and as Jim went overboard on one side and I on the other, she smashed right through the raft.

I dived—and I aimed to find the bottom, too. A thirty-foot wheel had to go over me, and I wanted it to have plenty of room. I could always stay under water a minute—this time I reckon I stayed under a minute and a half. Then I bounced for the top in a hurry, for I was nearly busting. I popped out to my armpits and snorted the water out of my nose, and puffed a bit.

I called out for Jim about a dozen times, but didn't get any answer. So I grabbed a plank that touched me while I was "treading water," and struck out for shore, shoving it ahead of me. I saw the drift of the current was toward the left-hand shore, so I went that way.

14 The Grangerfords Take Me In

I made a safe landing and climbed up the bank. It was so dark I could see only a little way ahead, but I went poking along over rough ground. Suddenly I saw a big old-fashioned double log house, right before me, and a lot of dogs jumped out and raised such a howling and barking I didn't dare move another peg. In about a minute somebody spoke out of a window, without putting his head out.

"Who is there?"

"George Jackson, sir. I'm only a boy."

"What do you want? What are you prowling around here this time of night for—hey?"

"I don't want anything, sir. I only want to go along by, but the dogs won't let me. I wasn't prowling around. I fell overboard off the steamboat."

"Oh, you did, did you? Look here, if you are telling the truth, you needn't be afraid—nobody will hurt you. But stand right where you are."

I heard the people stirring around in the house now, and saw a light. The man cried out:

"Snatch that light away, Betsy, you old fool. Put it on the floor behind the front door. Bob, are you and Tom at your places by the door?"

"All ready."

"Now, George Jackson, do you know the Shepherdsons?"

"No, sir; I never heard of them."

"Well, that may be so, and it may not be. Now step forward, and don't hurry—come mighty slow. If there's anybody with you, let him keep back, or he'll be shot. Come along now—come slow—push the door open yourself—just enough to squeeze in—"

I took one slow step at a time. There wasn't a sound, only I could hear my heart. The dogs kept still too, but they waited right behind me. I heard the people inside unlocking and unbarring the door. I put my hand on it and pushed a little. Somebody said:

"There, that's enough—put your head in."

I did, but I judged they would take it off. The candle was on the floor, and there stood three big men with guns pointed at me. The oldest was gray, and about sixty. The other two thirty or more—all fine, handsome men. The old gentleman said:

"There, I reckon it's all right. Come in."

They locked and barred the door as soon as I was in. Then they picked up the candle and took a good look at me.

"Why, *he* ain't no Shepherdson—no Shepherdson about him."

Then the old man said he hoped I wouldn't mind being searched for arms—only to make sure. He didn't pry into my pockets, only felt outside, and said it was all right. Then the sweetest old gray-headed lady comes up.

"Why, bless you, Saul, the poor thing is wet as he can be. And maybe he's hungry."

"True for you, Rachel—I forgot."

"Betsy," the old lady says, "you fly around and get him something to eat as quick as you can, poor thing. And one of you go up and wake Buck and tell him—oh, here he is now. Buck, take this little stranger and get the wet clothes off him and give him some of yours."

Buck looked about as old as I was—thirteen or fourteen, though he was a little bigger. He was gaping, digging one fist into his eyes, frowzy-headed, and he was dragging a gun.

"Ain't they no Shepherdsons around?"

They said, no, it was a false alarm.

"If they had been, I'd have got one."

They all laughed, and Bob said:

"Why, Buck, they might have scalped us all, you've been so slow coming."

"Well, nobody called me. I'm always kept down. I don't get any show."

"Never mind, Buck, my boy," said the old man. "You'll have show enough all in good time. Don't you fret about that. Go along with you now, and do as your mother told you."

When we got upstairs to Buck's room, he found me a shirt and pants, and I put them on. He asked me what my name was, but before I could tell him he started to tell me about a bluejay and a young rabbit he had caught. Then he asked me where Moses was when the candle went out. I said I didn't know.

"Well, guess," he said.

"But I don't know where he was. Where was he?"

"Why, he was in the *dark!*"

"Well, if you already know, why ask me?"

"Why, blame it, it's a riddle, don't you see? Say, how long are you going to stay here? You got to stay always. We can have booming times. Do you own a dog? My dog will go in the river and bring out chips that you throw in. Are you all ready to go down? Come along, old hoss."

While I was eating they asked me questions. I told them how all my family had lived on a little farm down in Arkansas—how my sister Mary Ann had run off and got married and never was heard of again—how Bill went to hunt them and he never was heard of again—how Tom and Mort died—how nobody was left but me and Pap, and he trimmed down to nothing on account of his trouble—how Pap died and I took what was left and started up the river on a steamboat, and fell overboard.

They said I could have a home there as long as I wanted it. After a while everybody went upstairs to bed. I went to bed with Buck. When I waked up next morning, I couldn't remember what I had told them my name was. So when Buck waked up, I said:

"Bet you can't spell my name."

"I bet you I can. G-e-o-r-g-e J-a-x-o-n—there now," he said.

"Well, you did. I didn't think you could."

It was a mighty nice family, and a mighty nice house too. In the parlor there was a big fireplace with brass dog-irons that could hold up a saw-log. On the mantel was a clock with a picture of a town on the lower half of the glass front. It was beautiful to hear that clock tick. As for striking, sometimes she would start in and strike a hundred and fifty before she got tuckered out.

Colonel Grangerford was a gentleman all over. He was well born, as the saying is, and that's worth as much in a man as it is in a horse. So the Widow Douglas said. Pap always said so too, though he was no more quality than a mudcat himself.

Every day Col. Grangerford was clean shaved, and every day of his life he put on a clean shirt and a fresh suit of white linen. He was as kind as he could be, but when he straightened himself up and the lightning begun to flicker from under his eyebrows, you wanted to climb a tree first, and find out what was the matter afterwards. Everybody was always good mannered where he was. When he and the old lady came down in the morning, all the family got out of their chairs to give them good day, and waited standing while they were being seated. Then Tom and Bob went to the sideboard and mixed glasses of bitters, and handed him a glass, bowed and said: "Our duty to you, sir, and madam." Col. Grangerford and the old lady bowed the least bit and said, "Thank you," and so they drank, all three.

Bob was the oldest and Tom was next—tall, beautiful men with very broad shoulders and brown faces and black hair and eyes. There used to be three more sons, but they got killed.

Miss Charlotte was twenty-five, proud and grand, but good as she could be when she wasn't stirred up. Her sister, Miss Sophia, was only twenty, and gentle and sweet like a dove.

The old gentleman owned a lot of farms and over a hundred slaves. Every white person had a servant. Mine had a very easy time, because I wasn't used to having anybody do anything for me. But Buck's was on the jump most of the time.

Sometimes a stack of people would come there, from ten or fifteen miles around, and stay five or six days. They would have parties on the river, and picnics in the woods daytimes, and balls at the house nights. The men brought their guns with them.

15 Why Harney Rode Away for His Hat

There was another clan around there—five or six families—mostly of the name of Shepherdson— all as well born and rich and grand as the tribe of Grangerfords.

One day when I was out hunting with Buck, close to a road, we heard a horse coming. We peeked through the leaves, and pretty soon a young man came galloping down the road. He was riding easy, and looking like a soldier, for he carried a gun. I had seen him before; he was young Harney Shepherdson. I heard Buck's gun go off beside me, and saw Harney's hat tumble off his head. He rode straight toward us and we started through the woods on a run. I kept looking over my shoulder to dodge any bullets that might be coming. I saw Harney cover Buck with his gun, but he didn't shoot. He turned and rode away—to get his hat, I reckon.

Soon as we stopped running I asked Buck why he wanted to kill him.

"On account of the feud," he said.

"What is a feud?"

"Don't you know what a feud is? Well, a feud is this way. A man has a quarrel with another man, and kills him. Then that other man's brother kills *him*. Then the brothers on both sides go after one

another. Then the *cousins* chip in. By and by everybody is killed off, and the feud is over. But it takes
a long time."

"Has this one been going on long, Buck?"

"Well, I should *say!* It started thirty years ago.
There was some trouble, about some land, I think,
then a lawsuit to settle it. Then the man that lost
the suit up and shot the man that won it."

"Who started the shooting—a Grangerford or a
Shepherdson?"

"Laws, how do *I* know. It was so long ago. Pa
knows, I reckon, and some of the other old people.
Pa has a few buckshot in him. Bob has been carved
up some with a knife, and Tom has been hurt once
or twice."

"Has anybody been killed this year, Buck?"

"Yes; we got one and they got one. About three
months ago, my cousin Bud, fourteen years old, was
riding through the woods without a gun—which was
blame foolishness. He hears a horse coming behind
him and sees old Baldy Shepherdson coming after
him with a gun in his hand and his white hair
a-flyin' in the wind. Bud thought he could outrun
him. So they had it nip and tuck for five miles or
more, the old man gaining all the time. At last Bud
saw it was no use. He stopped and faced around so
as to have the bullet holes in front. And the old man
rode up and shot him down. But he didn't get to enjoy
his luck for long. Inside of a week our folks laid *him*
out."

"I reckon that old man was a coward, Buck."

"Not by a blame sight. There ain't a coward
among the Shepherdsons—not a one. Why, that old
man kept up a fight one day for half an hour against
three Grangerfords, and won out, too. He lit off his

horse and got behind a woodpile, but the Grangerfords stayed on their horses and capered around the old man and peppered away at him. And he peppered away at them. He and his horse went home pretty leaky, but the Grangerfords had to be *carried* home. One of them was dead and another died the next day. No sir; the Shepherdsons don't breed cowards."

When we got home and told the old gentleman about it, his eyes blazed a minute. Then his face smoothed down, and he said, kind of gentle:

"I don't like shooting from behind a bush. Why didn't you step into the road, my boy?"

"The Shepherdsons don't, father. They always take advantage."

Miss Charlotte held her head up like a queen while Buck was telling his tale, and her eyes snapped. The two young men looked dark, but didn't say anything. Miss Sophia turned pale.

The next Sunday we all went to church. The men took their guns along, and kept them between their knees or stood them handy against the wall. The preaching was all about brotherly love. Everybody said it was a good sermon.

About an hour after dinner everybody was dozing around, some in their chairs and some in their rooms, and it got to be pretty dull. I judged maybe I would take a nap myself, and went upstairs. Miss Sophia was standing in her door waiting for me. She asked me if I would do something for her and not tell anybody. I said I would. She said she had left her Testament on the seat at church, and would I go there and get it for her. I said I would.

I found the Testament, and a little piece of paper in it, with "Half past two" written on it. When I got home and went upstairs, Miss Sophia was at her door waiting. She looked in the Testament and found the paper, and looked glad when she read it. Then she grabbed me and squeezed me and said I was the best boy in the world, and not to tell anybody.

I went off down toward the river. Pretty soon my servant comes running up behind me, and says:

"Mars George, if you'll come down into de swamp I'll show you a whole stack of water-moccasins."

I thought, that is mighty curious; he said that yesterday. He ought to know nobody loves water-moccasins enough to go around hunting for them. What is he up to, anyway? So I said:

"All right! trot ahead."

I followed, and soon he struck out over the swamp, and waded ankle deep till we reached a flat dry land, thick with trees, bushes, and vines. He stopped and said:

"You shove right in dah, just a few steps, Mars George. Dah is where dey is. I don't keer to see 'em no mo'."

I poked into the place a few steps, and—by jings, there was my old Jim! He nearly cried, he was so glad, but he wasn't surprised to see me. He said he had come out of the river not far behind me, that night. He had heard me yell every time, but didn't dare answer, because he didn't want anybody to pick him up and take him into slavery again. "I got hurt a little, and couldn't catch up with you. When I see dat house, I went slow. When de dogs quieted down I knowed you was in de house. So I struck out for de woods to wait for day. Next day some of de field slaves found me and showed me dis place, whah de dogs can't track me on account of the water. Dey brings me truck to eat every night, and tells me how you is gettin' along."

"Why didn't you tell my Jack to bring me here sooner?"

"I have been busy nights, patchin' up de raft. She was tore up a good deal. But now she is all fixed up again good as new, and I been a-buyin' pots and pans, and a canoe, and a lot of stuff we lost."

"How did you get hold of the raft again, Jim?"

"Some of de folks found her caught on a snag, and dey hid her amongst de willows. Dey is mighty good to me, dese people is. Dat Jack is good and smart."

"Yes, he is. He told me to come here and he would show me a lot of water-moccasins. If anything happens, he can say he never saw us together."

I don't want to say much about the next day. I wish I had never gone ashore that night to see such things. I never can get them out of my mind—lots of times I dream about them.

Well, I waked up early, and was going to turn over and go to sleep again, when I noticed how still it was—nobody stirring. Next I saw that Buck was up and gone. I got up and went down stairs—nobody around. Everything as still as a mouse. Just the same outside. What could it mean? Down by the woodpile I found my Jack and asked him what it was all about.

"Don't you know, Mars George? Miss Sophia has run off to get married to dat young Harney Shepherdson. She went in de night—nobody knows just when. But when de family found out about it, such another hurryin' up guns and horses you never see! De women folks is gone to stir up de relations, and old Mars Saul and de boys rode up de river road to try to find dat young man and kill him befo' he can get across de river with Miss Sophia."

I took up the river road as hard as I could put. By and by I begin to hear guns a good way off. When I got in sight of the store and the woodpile where the steamboats land, I climbed up into a cottonwood and watched. Four or five men went cavorting around on horses before the log store, cussing and yelling, and trying to get a shot at two boys squatting behind the woodpile alongside the steamboat landing. By and by up gets one of the boys, draws a steady bead over the woodpile, and drops one of the men out of his saddle. All the other men jumped off their horses and went to pick up the hurt one and carried him into the store. That minute the two boys started on the run, and got behind a woodpile in front of my tree.

One of the boys was Buck, and the other was a slim young chap about nineteen years old. After a while the men came out of the store and rode away. I called out to Buck. He told me to watch out sharp for the men—said they were up to some devilment—wouldn't be gone long. Then he began to cry and rip, and said he and his cousin Joe would make up for this day yet. He said his father and his two brothers had been killed, and two or three of the enemy. Said they should have waited for their relations—the Shepherdsons had been too strong for them—said the Shepherdsons had laid for them in ambush.

I asked him what had become of young Harney and Miss Sophia. He said they had got across the river. I was glad of that, but the way Buck did take on because he hadn't killed Harney that day he shot at him!

All of a sudden three or four guns went bang! bang! bang! The men had slipped around through the woods and come in from behind. The boys jumped for the river—both of them hurt—and went swimming down the current. The men went running along the bank shooting at them. It made me so sick I almost fell out of the tree.

I stayed in the tree for hours, afraid to come down. Sometimes I heard guns away off in the woods. Twice I saw little gangs of men gallop past the log store with guns, so I reckoned the trouble was still going on.

I was mighty downhearted. I made up my mind I would never go near the house again. Maybe I was to blame, somehow. That piece of paper I took to Miss Sophia meant she was to meet Harney somewhere at half-past two and run off. Maybe I should have told her father about that piece of paper, and then maybe he would have locked her up, and this awful mess wouldn't ever have happened.

I climbed down the tree and crept along down the river bank. I found two bodies at the edge of the water and I tugged till I got them ashore. Then I covered up their faces. I cried when I was covering up Buck's face, for he had been mighty good to me. Then I went away from there as fast as I could.

16 *Royalty Comes Aboard*

By this time it was dark. I struck through the woods and made for the swamp. Jim wasn't on his island in the swamp, so I tramped off in a hurry, looking for the creek where the raft was. I crowded through the willows, red-hot to jump aboard and get out of that awful country. The raft was gone! My soul, but I was scared. I raised a yell, and Jim's voice answered not far off:

"Good land, is dat you, honey? Don't make no noise."

I hurried along the bank and got aboard. Jim grabbed me and hugged me.

"Lawd bless you, child, I was right down sho' you was dead again. Jack's been here, and he reckoned you had been shot, 'cause you didn't come home. I was jist dis minute a-startin' de raft down to de river. I was a-gettin' all ready to shove out as soon as Jack come to tell me for certain you is dead."

I said, "All right—good. They won't find me, and they'll think I've been killed, and floated down the river—something is up there to help them think so. Don't lose any time, Jim, but shove off for the big water as fast as you can."

I didn't feel easy till the raft was two miles below there, and out in the middle of the Mississippi. Then we hung up our signal lantern and judged that we would be safe and free once more. I hadn't had a bite to eat since yesterday, so Jim got out some food, and while we had supper we talked.

I was glad to get away from the feuds, and Jim was glad to get away from the island in the swamp. We said there was no home like a raft—you feel so free and easy on a raft.

Two or three days and nights slid by, quiet and lovely. It was a monstrous big river down there, sometimes a mile and a half wide. We floated along at night, and tied up in the daytime. Mornings, the first thing we would see, looking away over the water, was a dull line. That was the woods on the other side. Then a pale place in the sky. Then the river wasn't black anymore, but gray. You can see little dark spots drifting along ever so far away, trading boats. And long black streaks, rafts. By and by you can see a streak on the water where a snag breaks the swift current. You see the mist curl up off the water. The east reddens up, and the river with it. Then the breeze springs up and comes fanning so cool and fresh and sweet to smell from the woods and flowers.

A little smoke wouldn't be noticed now. So we would take some fish off the line and cook up a hot breakfast. Afterwards we would watch the lonesome river lazy along, and by and by lazy off to sleep.

Soon as it was night, out we shoved. When we got her to about the middle, we let her float wherever the current wanted her.

One morning about daybreak I took the canoe and crossed over to the main shore, about two hundred yards. I paddled up a creek among the cypress woods to look for some berries. Suddenly here come a couple of men as fast as they can foot it. I thought I was a goner—they must be after me, or maybe Jim. But they begged me to save *their* lives. Said they hadn't been doing anything, and were being chased for it. Said men and dogs were coming. They jumped right into the canoe, and I lit out for our towhead. In a few minutes we heard the dogs baying and the men shouting. But by the time we had left the woods and struck the river, everything was quiet. We paddled over to the towhead and hid in the cottonwoods.

One of these fellows was about seventy. He had a bald head and gray whiskers. He wore an old battered hat, and a greasy woolen shirt, and ragged old jeans stuffed into his boot-tops. The other fellow was about thirty, and dressed about as bad. Both of them had big, fat, dirty carpet-bags.*

After breakfast we talked. The first thing that came out was that these two chaps didn't know one another.

"Young man," said the old one, "what is your line of work—mainly?"

"Printer by trade. Do a little in patent medicines—theater actor—sling a lecture sometimes. Oh, I do lots of things—anything that comes handy, so long as it's not work. What's your line?"

"I've done a lot in the doctoring way. Laying on of hands is the best thing I do—cure cancer and such things. And I can tell a fortune pretty well, when I have somebody along to find out the facts for me. Preaching is my line, too, and working in camp meetings."

Nobody said anything for a while. Then the young man heaved a sigh and said, very sadly:

---

* A kind of handbag, especially one made of carpet material.

"Gentlemen, I will tell you the truth—for I feel I can trust you. By rights I am a duke!"

Jim's eyes bugged out when he heard that, and I reckon mine did too.

"Yes, my great-grandfather was the eldest son of the Duke of Bridgewater. He fled to this country to breathe the pure air of freedom. The second son took the titles and the estates. But I am the rightful Duke of Bridgewater. And here am I, thrown out on the cold world, living on a raft, with thieves and law-breakers!"

Jim pitied him and so did I. But the old man said:

"Looky here, Bilgewater, you're not the only person that has been wronged and put out of a high place. I've had a secret birth too. I'm the Dauphin of France!"

The duke said, "You are what?"

"I am the lost Dauphin, Looy the Seventeen."

"You! At your age! No! You mean you are the late Charlemagne.* You must be six or seven hundred years old, at the very least."

"Trouble has done it, Bilgewater. Trouble has brought these gray hairs and this early baldness. Yes, gentlemen, you see before you, in rags and misery, the rightful King of France."

It didn't take me long to make up my mind that they were not kings and dukes, but just low-down humbugs. But I kept it to myself. If they wanted us to call them kings and dukes, I didn't object, so long as it kept peace in the family. I learned from living with Pap that the best way to get along with his kind is to let them have their own way.

---

* Charles the Great, or Charles I (742–814), king of the Franks.

They asked us a lot of questions—Why did we try to keep the raft hid?—Why did we travel only at night?—Was Jim a runaway slave?

"Goodness sakes," I said, "would a runaway slave run *south?*"

No, they said, he wouldn't. But I had to account for things some way. So I said:

"My folks lived in Pike County in Missouri. They all died off but me and Pa and my brother Ike. Pa decided to go down and live with Uncle Ben, forty miles below Orleans. But when Pa squared up his debts all we had left was sixteen dollars and our Jim. So we started south on a raft. A steamboat went over the raft one night. Pa was drunk and Ike was only four years old, so they didn't come up again. That left only Jim and me. Then people got to coming out in skiffs and trying to take Jim away from me. They said they believed he was a runaway. So we don't travel in the daytime now. Nights they don't bother us."

Well, the king got out an old deck of cards, and he and the duke played seven-up awhile, five cents a game. Then they got tired of that, and said they would work out some plans.

The duke opened up his carpet-bag and brought out a lot of little printed bills, and read them out loud. One bill said the great Doctor Armand of Paris would "lecture and furnish charts of character at twenty-five cents apiece." The duke said he was Doctor Armand. Another bill said he was the "world-famous actor Garrick the Younger of London." In other bills he had a lot of other names and could do wonderful things.

"But acting is the best thing I do. Have you ever been an actor, Royalty?"

"No," said the king.

"You shall, then, before you're a day older," said the duke. "The first good town we come to, we'll hire a hall and do the balcony scene in *Romeo and Juliet.* How does that strike you?"

"I'm in for anything that will pay, Bilgewater. But I don't know anything about play-acting. Do you reckon you can teach me?"

"Easy!"

So the duke told him all about who Romeo was and who Juliet was. He said he would be Romeo and the king could be Juliet.

"But if Juliet is such a young gal, my bald head and my white whiskers will look odd on her, maybe."

"Don't you worry. These country jakes won't ever think of that. Besides, you will be in costume. Juliet is in the balcony, enjoying the moonlight before she goes to bed. Here is the costume for the part."

He took out a long white cotton night shirt and a ruffled night cap. Then the duke got out his book and read the parts over. All the time he was reading he pranced around and acted to show the king how it had to be done. Then he handed the book to the king and told him to learn his part by heart.

The duke said he had thought up a way we could travel by daylight, without danger to Jim. He said he would fix the thing up at the town we would be coming to next. It was a little one-horse town three miles down the river. When we got there, Jim said I had better go ashore with the two, to buy some coffee.

When we landed not a soul was stirring. Streets empty, and dead still, like Sunday. We found an old slave sunning himself in a back yard, and he said everybody that wasn't too sick or too old had gone to camp meeting, about two miles back in the woods.

The duke said what he was after was a printing office. We found it, a little place up over a carpenter shop—carpenters and printers all gone to the meeting, and no doors locked. It was a dirty, littered-up place, and had ink marks, and handbills with pictures of horses and runaway slaves on them, all over the walls. The duke shed his coat and said he was all right now. He set up and printed off a handbill with a picture of a runaway slave with a bundle on a stick over his shoulder, and "$200 reward" under it. The reading was all about Jim, and just described him to a dot. It said he had run away from St. Jacques' plantation, forty miles below New Orleans, last winter, and likely went north, and whoever would catch him and bring him back could have the reward and expenses.

"Now," said the duke, "after tonight we can run in the daytime, if we want to. Whenever we see anybody coming we can tie Jim hand and foot with a rope, and lay him in the wigwam and show this handbill and say we caught him up the river and are going down to get the reward."

The king got directions of the camp-meeting, about two miles back in the woods. He said he reckoned he would go and work that camp-meeting for all it was worth, and I might go too.

We got there in about half an hour, fairly dripping, for it was a most awful hot day. People had come from twenty miles around—the woods full of wagons, and teams hitched everywhere, feeding and stomping to keep off the flies. They had sheds made out of poles and roofed over with branches, where they sold lemonade and gingerbread, and piles of watermelons, green corn, and such truck.

The preaching was going on under the same kinds of sheds, only bigger, to hold the crowds of people. The benches, made out of slabs of logs with holes bored in the round side to drive sticks into for legs, didn't have any backs. The preachers had high platforms to stand on at one end of the sheds.

The women had on sun-bonnets, and some had linsey-woolsey dresses, some gingham, and a few of the young ones had on calico. Some of the young men were barefooted, and some of the children didn't have on any clothes but a tow-linen shirt. The old women kept busy knitting, and the young folks courted on the sly.

At the first shed we stopped at, the preacher was lining out a hymn. He lined out two lines, everybody sung it, then he lined out two more lines for them to sing. It was kind of grand to hear so many singing in such a rousing way.

The people woke up more and more, and sung louder and louder. Toward the end, some began to groan, and some to shout. Then the preacher went to preaching, and in earnest too. He went weaving first to one side of the platform and then to the other. Then he would lean down over the front of it, with his arms and his body going all the time, shouting his words out with all his might, the people all the time shouting out, "Glory—amen!" and groaning and crying. The preacher went right on:

"Oh, come to the mourner's bench! Come, black with sin! Come, sick and sore! Come, lame and halt and blind! Come, pore and needy, sunk in shame!

Come, all that is worn and soiled and suffering! Come with a broken spirit! Come in your rags and sin and dirt! The waters that cleanse is free, the door of heaven stands open—oh, enter in and be at rest!"

After a while you couldn't make out what the preacher said any more, on account of the shouting

and crying. Folks got up everywhere in the crowd, and worked their way by main strength to the mourner's bench, with tears running down their faces. When all the mourners had got up there to the front benches, they sung and shouted and flung themselves down on the ground, just crazy and wild.

Well, the first thing I knew the king got going, and you could hear him above everybody. Next he went charging up onto the platform, and the preacher begged him to speak to the people, and he did. He said he was a pirate—and had been a pirate for thirty years out in the Indian Ocean. His crew was thinned out last spring in a fight, and he was home now to take out some fresh men. But thanks to goodness he was robbed last night and put ashore off a steamboat without a cent. He was glad of it, because now he was a changed man, and happy for the first time in his life. Poor as he was, he was going to start right off and work his way back to the Indian Ocean. There he would put in the rest of his life trying to turn the pirates away from evil. It would take him a long time to get there without money, but he would get there somehow.

Then he busted into tears, and so did everybody else. Then somebody called out, "Take up a collection for him—take up a collection!" Half a dozen made a jump to do it, but somebody said, "Let *him* pass the hat around!"

So the king went all through the crowd holding out his hat, swabbing his eyes, and blessing and praising and thanking the people for being so good to him and the poor pirates out in the Indian Ocean.

When we got back to the raft and he counted up, he found he had collected eighty-seven dollars and seventy-five cents.

17 *Trouble in Arkansas*

Next morning we started out in broad daylight. After breakfast the king took a seat on the corner of the raft, pulled off his boots, and let his legs dangle in the water. Then he lit his pipe and went to getting his *Romeo and Juliet* by heart.

Then the duke went to practicing it with him. The duke had to teach him how to say every speech.

"You mustn't bellow out *Romeo!* that way, like a bull. You must say it soft and loving—R-o-o-meo! Juliet is a dear sweet mere child of a girl. She wouldn't bray like a jackass."

So he went to marching up and down, thinking, and frowning. Then he would hoist up his eyebrows. Next he would squeeze his hand on his forehead and stagger back and kind of moan.

Well, all that day we floated along, and the raft was a lively place, acting going on all the time. That night we tied the raft to the shore and slept. The duke said the play was ready to give.

Next morning we came in sight of a little one-horse town and tied the raft about a mile above, in the mouth of a creek, behind some trees. All of us but Jim went to town to see if there was any chance for our show. We struck it lucky. It was circus day, and there would be a crowd. Country people were already coming in. The circus would leave before night, so our show would have a pretty good chance.

The duke hired the court-house, and we went around and stuck up our bills. They read like this:

Shakspere Revival!
For One Night Only!
The World-Famous Actor,
David Garrick the Younger,
of London,
and
Edmund Kean the Elder, of London!
The Balcony Scene
in
Romeo and Juliet!
Romeo .... Mr. Garrick
Juliet .... Mr. Kean
Assisted by the whole strength of the company!
New Costumes, new scenery, new appointments!
Admission 25 cents   Children and servants 10 cents

Then we went loafing around town. The houses were old shacks that had never been painted, set up on stilts to be out of reach of water when the river overflowed. Each house was fenced in with a garden spot, but the gardens had nothing in them but weeds and sunflowers, and ash piles, and old curled-up boots, and pieces of bottles. Some of the fences had been white-washed a long time ago—the duke said maybe in Columbus's time.

All the stores had white domestic awnings in front. Loafers roosted under them all day long, whittling and chewing tobacco, and yawning and stretching. They called one another Bill, Buck, Hank, Joe, and Andy, and talked lazy and drawly with a lot of cusswords. What you would hear them say most was:

"Gimme a chaw of tobacker, Hank."

"Can't, I ain't got but one chaw left. Ask Bill."

The street was just mud—mud as black as tar, a foot deep in some places, and two or three inches deep in *all* places. You would see a muddy sow come lazing along and whallop herself right down in the street. Pretty soon a loafer would sing out: "Hi! sick him, Tige!" Away the sow would go squealing, with a dog or two swinging to each ear. The loafers would stand up to watch the thing out of sight and laugh at the fun. Then they would settle back till there was a dog fight.

By noon the crowd was thick, and more people coming all the time. By and by somebody said:

"Here comes old Boggs!—in for his little old monthly drunk. Here he comes boys!"

All the loafers looked glad. One of them said: "Wonder who he's going to chew up this time." Another one said: "I wish old Boggs would threaten me. Then I'd know I wasn't going to die soon."

Boggs comes tearing along on his horse, weaving about in his saddle, and yelling like an Injun:

"Clear the track thar. I am on the war-path, and the price of coffins is goin' up."

He was over fifty years old, and had a very red face. Everybody yelled and laughed at him. He sassed back and said he would attend to them, and lay them out in their turn. Then he saw me and rode up and said:

"Whar you come from, boy? You prepared to die?"

I was scared, but a man said:

"He always carries on like that when he's drunk. The best natured old fool in Arkansas. Never hurt nobody—drunk or sober."

Boggs rode up before the biggest store in town, bent his head down to look under the awning and yelled:

"Come out here, Sherburn! Come out and meet the man you swindled. You are the hound I'm after!"

He went on calling Sherburn everything he could lay his tongue to. The whole street was packed with people listening and laughing. By and by a proud looking man stepped out of the store. They said it was Colonel Sherburn. He was the best dressed man in that town. He said to Boggs, calm and slow:

"I'm tired of this. I'll endure it till one o'clock— no longer. If you open your mouth against me only once after that time you can't travel so far but I'll find you."

He turned and went back in. The crowd looked sober, nobody was laughing. Boggs rode off abusing Sherburn as loud as he could yell. Pretty soon back he comes, and stopped before the store, still keeping it up. Some men tried to get him to shut up, but he wouldn't. They told him it would be one o'clock in fifteen minutes, and he *must* go home right away. They tried to coax him off his horse so they could lock him up and get him sober. But it was no use— up the street he would tear again, and give Sherburn another cussing.

I walked down the street a way and stopped. In five or ten minutes here comes Boggs again, but not on his horse. He was reeling along bareheaded, with a friend on each side holding his arms and hurrying him along. He was quiet and looked uneasy. He wasn't hanging back, but was doing some of the hurrying himself. Somebody called out:

"Boggs!"

It was Colonel Sherburn. He was standing still

in the street, and had a pistol raised in his right hand, tilted up toward the sky.

Boggs and the men turned round to see who called. When they saw the pistol, the two men let go of Boggs and jumped to one side. The pistol-barrel comes down slow and steady to a level. Boggs throws up both hands and says, "Oh Lord, don't shoot." Bang! goes the first shot, and he staggers back, clawing at the air. Bang! goes the second shot, and he tumbles backward to the ground, heavy and solid, his arms spread out.

Colonel Sherburn tossed his pistol onto the ground and turned and walked off. Some men took Boggs to a little drug store, the whole crowd following. I rushed and got a good place at the window. They laid him on the floor and put a large Bible under his head, and another spread open on his breast. He made about a dozen long gasps, his breast lifting the Bible up and down. After that he was still, he was dead.

The crowd was pushing and shoving to get at the window to have a look, the people behind saying:

"Say, now, you've looked long enough, fellows. It ain't fair for you to stay thar all the time and never give nobody else a chance to see."

Well, by and by somebody said Sherburn ought to be lynched. In about a minute everybody was saying it. So away they went, mad and yelling and snatching down every clothes-line they passed. They swarmed up to Sherburn's fence, and somebody yelled:

"Tear down the fence!"

There was a ripping and smashing, and down she goes. The crowd rolled in like a wave. Just then Sherburn stepped out on the roof of his front porch, with a double-barrel gun in his hand. The racket stopped, and the crowd sucked back. Sherburn let his eye run along the crowd. They dropped their gaze and looked sneaky. Then Sherburn laughed a scornful way and said:

"The idea of *you* thinking you had pluck enough to lynch a *man*. Because you are brave enough to tar and feather poor out-cast women that come along here, you think you have grit enough to lay your hands on a *man*. Why a *man* is safe in the hands of ten thousand of your kind—as long as it is daytime and you are not behind him. I know you clear through. The pitifulest thing out is a mob. That is what an army is—a mob. They don't fight with courage born in them, but with courage borrowed from their mass and from their officers. But a mob without any *man* at the head of it is *beneath* pity. Now you drop your tails and go home and crawl in a hole. If any real lynching is to be done, it'll be done in the dark, southern fashion. And when they come, they'll bring their masks and have a *man* along. Now *leave*."

He tossed his gun up across his left arm, and the crowd washed back, and broke apart, and went tearing off every which way. I left too, because I didn't want to stay either.

18 The Circus and the Royal Nonesuch

I went to the circus and loafed around the backside till the watchman went by. Then I dived in under the tent. I had some money, but I reckoned I better save it. No telling how soon you are going to need it, away from home and among strangers. I'm not against spending money on a circus when there's no other way to get in, but there's no use *wasting* on them.

It was a real bully circus. It was a splendid sight to see them all come riding in, two and two, gentleman and lady side by side, the men resting their hands on their thighs so easy. There must have been twenty of them. And every lady with a lovely complexion and perfectly beautiful. They looked just like a gang of sure enough queens. Then one by one they got up and stood on their horses and went weaving around the ring, so gentle and wavy and graceful. The men looked ever so tall and airy and straight with their heads bobbing and skimming along away up there under the tent roof, and every lady looking like the most lovely parasol with her rose-leafy dress flapping soft and silky around her hips.

Then faster and faster they went, all of them dancing, first one foot in the air and then the other. The horses went leaning more and more, the ringmaster cracking his whip and shouting "Hi!—hi!" And so, one after the other, they skipped off, into the ring and made the sweetest bow and went running out. Everybody clapped and went wild.

And all the time the clown was carrying on so it almost killed the people. The ringmaster couldn't say a word but the clown was back at him quick as a wink. How he ever *could* think of so many funny things to say and so sudden and so pat, was what I couldn't understand. I couldn't have thought of them in a year.

By and by a drunk man tried to get into the ring—said he wanted to ride—said he could ride as well as anybody. The ringmaster argued and tried to keep him out, but he wouldn't listen. The whole show had to come to a standstill. Then the people hollered at him and made fun of him. That made him mad, and he commenced to rip and tear. That stirred up the people, and a lot of men commenced to pile down off of the benches and went swarming out towards the ring, saying, "Knock him down! Throw him out!" Some women screamed. Then the ringmaster made a little speech. He said he hoped there wouldn't be any disturbance. If the man would promise not to make any more trouble, he would let him ride—if he could stay on the horse. So everybody laughed and said all right, and the man got on. The minute he was on, the horse began to rip and tear and jump around. It was all two circus men could do to hang on to the bridle. The drunk man grabbed the horse around the neck to hold on, and his heels went flying in the air at every jump. The whole crowd stood up and shouted and laughed till the tears rolled down. Then, in spite of all the circus men could do, the horse broke loose. Away he went, round and round the ring, with that sot hanging to his neck, with first one leg nearly to the ground on one side and then the other on the other side. The people just went crazy.

It wasn't funny to me, for I was all a-tremble at his danger. But pretty soon he struggled up and grabbed the bridle, reeling this way and that. The next minute he dropped the bridle and stood up on the horse! And the horse going like a house afire all the time. He stood up there and went sailing around as easy as if he never had been drunk in his life. Then he began to pull off his clothes and sling them. He shed them so fast they seemed to clog the air. Altogether he shed seventeen suits. And there he was, slim and handsome, and dressed the gaudiest and prettiest you ever saw. Then he lit into that horse with his whip and made him fairly hum. Finally he skipped off the horse, made a bow and danced off to the dressing room. Everybody was just howling with pleasure and surprise.

When the ringmaster saw he had been fooled he *was* the sickest man you ever saw. I felt sheepish enough to be so taken in, but I wouldn't have been in that ringmaster's place for a thousand dollars. Why, it was one of his own men! He had got up that joke and never let on to anybody.

Well, that night we had our show. Only about twelve people there—just enough to pay expenses. And they laughed all the time, and that made the duke mad. Everybody left before the show was over, but one boy who was asleep. So the duke said these

Arkansas lunkheads couldn't come up to Shake-speare. What they wanted was something worse than low comedy. He said he could judge their style.

Next morning he got some big sheets of wrapping paper and some black paint, and made big handbills that said:

At The Court House!
Three Nights Only!!
The World-Famous Actors
David Garrick the Younger
and
Edmund Kean the Elder
of London,
In Their Thrilling Tragedy
The Royal Nonesuch
Admission 50 cents
LADIES AND CHILDREN NOT ADMITTED

"There," he said, "if that last line won't bring them in, I don't know Arkansas!"

We stuck the showbills up all over the village, and that night the house was jammed full of men in no time. When the place couldn't hold any more, the duke quit tending the door and went around the back way, and walked out on the stage. He stood up before the curtain and made a little speech. He praised up the show, said it was the most thrillingest one that ever was. He bragged about Edmund Kean the Elder, who was to play the main part in it. At last, when he had got everybody's interest high enough, he rolled up the curtain.

The next minute the king pranced out on all fours, naked, painted all over, ring-streaked and striped, in all sorts of colors. It was just wild, but it was awful funny. The people 'most killed themselves laughing at the king capering around on the stage. And when he capered off behind the scenes, they roared and clapped and stormed and haw-hawed, till he had to come back and do it all again. Then they made him do it another time. It would make a cow laugh to see the shines that old idiot cut.

Then the duke let the curtain down and bowed to the people. He said he was glad the show had pleased them, and would they tell their friends to come and see it tomorrow night. Twenty people yelled out:

"What! Is it over? Is that all?"

The duke said yes. Then everybody cried out, "Sold!" and they rose up mad, and started for the stage. But a big fine-looking man jumped on a bench and shouted:

"Hold on! Just a word, gentlemen." They stopped to listen. "We are sold—badly sold. But we don't want to be the laughing-stock of the whole town. Let's all go out of here quiet, and talk this show up, and sell the rest of the town. Then we'll all be in the same boat. Isn't that sensible!"

"You bet it is—the judge is right."

"All right then—not a word about being sold. Go along home, and advise everybody to come and see the show tomorrow night."

The next night the house was jammed again, and we sold this crowd the same way. The third night the house was crammed again. I stood by the duke at the door, and saw the people go in. Every man had his pockets bulging, or something muffled up under his coat. I smelt sickly eggs by the barrel, and rotten cabbages, and if I know the smell of a dead cat, sixty-four of them went in.

Well, when the place was full, the duke handed a quarter to a fellow to tend door for him a minute. Then he started around for the stage door, I after him. The minute we turned the corner he said:

"Walk fast now till you get away from the town, and then strike out for the raft like the dickens was after you."

We both did, and got to the raft at the same time. In less than two seconds the raft was gliding down stream, dark and still. I reckoned the poor king was in for a bad time, left to face all the people alone. But nothing of the sort—pretty soon he crawled out from under the wigwam, and said:

"Well, how did the show pan out this time, duke?" He hadn't been in town at all.

We didn't show a light until ten miles below the town. Then we lit up and had supper. The king and the duke fairly laughed their bones loose over the way they had served the people in the town. The duke said:

"Greenhorns, flatheads! *I* knowed they would lay for us the third night. They'd think, 'Now it is *our* turn.' I *would* give anything to know how they're taking it."

The king and the duke took in $465 in the three nights. I never saw money hauled in by the wagonload like that before.

By and by when Jim heard them snoring, he said:

"Don't it surprise you de way dem kings carries on, Huck?"

"No," I said. "I reckon they're all alike."

"But, Huck, dese kings of ourn is regular rapscallions. Dat is just what dey is, Huck—dey is regular rapscallions."

"That's what I said. All kings are mostly rapscallions, as far as I can make out."

"Is dat so?"

"You read about them once—you'll see. Look at Henry the Eighth. This one is a Sunday-school superintendent to *him*. My, you ought to have seen old Henry the Eighth when he was in bloom. He *was* a blossom. He used to marry a new wife every day, and chop her head off next morning. And he made every one of them tell him a tale every night, and kept that up till he had a thousand and one tales. Then he put them all in a book and called it Domesday Book. You don't know kings, Jim; but I know them, and this old rip of ours is one of the cleanest I ever heard of in history. Well, King Henry, he took a notion to get up some trouble in this country. He heaves all the tea in Boston harbor overboard, and whacks out a declaration of independence, and dares them to come on. That was the kind of bug Henry was. He would have fooled that town a heap worse than our kings did. You have to make allowances for kings. Take them all around, they are a mighty ornery lot."

"But dis one do *smell* so like de nation, Huck!"

"Well, they all do, Jim. We can't help the way a king smells."

"Now de duke, he is a likely man in some ways."

"This one is a hard lot for a duke. When he's drunk a near-sighted man couldn't tell him from a king."

"Well, anyways, I don't hanker for no mo' of 'em. Dese is all I can stand."

"I feel the same way, Jim. But we have them on our hands. Sometimes I wish we could hear of a country that is out of kings."

19 The King Turns Parson

One day we tied up under a little willow towhead out in the middle of the river. There was a village on each side of us, and the duke and the king got busy making plans to work these towns. Jim spoke to the duke and said he hoped it wouldn't take long. He said it was mighty tiresome to be kept all day in the wigwam tied with a rope. You see, when we left him all alone, we tied him with a rope so he would look like a captured runaway slave if anybody happened to come on him.

The duke said he'd fix that. He dressed Jim up in a long calico gown and put a wig and whiskers on him. Then he took his theater paint and painted Jim's face and hands a dull solid blue. He looked like a man that had been drowned nine days. Then the duke put a sign on the wigwam:

Sick Arab—but harmless when not out of his head.

Jim was satisfied. He said it was better than being left tied up for hours, and trembling at every sound.

The king and the duke couldn't hit on any plan to work the towns. It wouldn't be safe to try the *Nonesuch* again; news of it might have worked down by this time. At last the duke said he'd work his brains an hour or two and see if he could turn up some plan. The king said he would drop over to the village on the other side and trust his luck to Providence—meaning the devil, I reckon.

He dressed up in store clothes, all black, and he looked real swell and starchy. When he took off his white beaver hat and made a bow and smiled, he looked so grand and good and pious, you would think he had walked right out of the ark.

There was a big steamboat at the shore about three miles above, taking on freight. The king said he would get on that steamboat and arrive in the village from St. Louis or Cincinnati. He told Jim to clean up the canoe and me to get my paddles ready.

I rowed up the river, close to the bank in easy water. Pretty soon we passed a nice, innocent-looking country fellow, carrying a couple of carpet-bags.

"Where are you bound for, young man?" called out the king.

"For the steamboat—going to Orleans."

"Get aboard," said the king. "Hold on a minute, my servant will help you with the bags. Jump out and help the gentleman, Adolphus"—meaning me.

I helped him in, and we all three started on again. The young chap said he was thankful for the ride; it was tough work toting his baggage on such a hot day. Then he said:

"When I first saw you I thought you might be Harvey Wilks. I said to myself, 'He almost got here on time.' Then I remembered he wouldn't be paddling *up* the river. You *ain't* him, are you?"

"No; my name is Alexander Blodgett—*Reverend* Blodgett, one of the Lord's poor servants. I'm sorry Mr. Wilks didn't arrive in time—I hope he didn't miss anything serious."

"He won't miss any property—he'll get that all right. But he missed seeing his brother Peter alive. Peter wanted so much to see Harvey before he died. He hadn't seen him since they were boys in England. He never had seen his brother William—the deaf and dumb one."

"Where was Harvey coming from?"

"Oh, he lives in England—preaches there—never been in this country. Only two of the brothers came to America—Peter and George—about forty years ago. George and his wife died and left three girls. Peter took care of them. Now he's gone, and the girls are left alone. Peter wouldn't make a will, but he left a letter for Harvey, telling where the money is and how he wanted the property divided up."

"How old are the girls?"

"Mary Jane is nineteen, Susan is fifteen, and Joanna about fourteen."

"Poor things! to be left alone in the cold world."

"Well, old Peter had friends, and they won't let them come to harm. There's Hobson, the Baptist preacher, and Deacon Lot Hovey, Ben Rucker, Abner Shackleford, Levi Bell, the lawyer, and Doctor Robinson, and the Widow Bartley."

Well, the king went on asking questions till he fairly emptied that young fellow. He inquired about everybody and everything in that blessed town.

"Was Peter Wilks well off?"

"Pretty well off. He had houses and land, and three or four thousand in cash hid somewhere."

"When did you say he died?"

"I didn't say, but it was last night."

"Funeral tomorrow, likely?"

"Yes, about the middle of the day."

When we struck the steamboat the king didn't

go aboard, but waited till the boat left. Then he said to me:

"Hustle back and fetch the duke up here, and the new carpet-bags. If he's gone over to the other side of the river, go after him. Shove along now."

I saw what *he* was up to. But I said nothing, of course.

When I got back with the duke, the king told him everything the young fellow had said. And all the time he tried to talk like an Englishman.

"Tell me, how are you on the deaf and dumb, Bilgewater?"

The duke said leave him alone for that, said he had played the part on the stage many a time.

We hid the canoe and waited until a steamboat came along. They hailed her and we got aboard and landed at the village. About two dozen men flocked to meet the boat. The king looked around and said:

"Can any of you tell me where Mr. Peter Wilks lives?"

They glanced at one another as much as to say, "Poor old Peter's brothers." Then one of them said kind of soft and gentle:

"The best we can do is to tell you where he *did* live. He died last night."

Sudden as winking that ornery old king went all to smash. He fell up against the man, put his chin on his shoulder, and cried down his back.

"Alas, our poor brother—gone and we never got to see him!"

Then he turned to the duke, blubbering, and made a lot of idiotic signs on his hands. Blamed if the duke didn't drop a carpet-bag and bust out a-crying. The men gathered around and said all sorts of kind things. They carried their carpet-bags up the hill for them. They told the king all about Peter's last hours, and the king told it all over again, on his hands, to the duke. It was enough to make a body ashamed of the human race.

When he got to the house the three girls came running to meet us. Mary Jane, the red-headed one, was most awful beautiful. Her face and eyes lit up like glory, she was so glad her uncles had come. Everybody cried for joy.

Then the king and the duke looked around and saw the coffin over in the corner on two chairs. They went and bent over and looked in, and bust out a-crying. They put their arms around each other's neck, and I never saw two men leak the way they did. Mind you, everybody there was doing the same. I never saw anything like it.

Then the king said how glad he would be if a few friends of his brother Peter would take supper there and keep watch that night with the ashes of the dead. He said he would name the ones his brother often wrote about: Reverend Mr. Hobson, Deacon Lot Hovey, Ben Rucker, Abner Shackleford, Levi Bell, Doctor Robinson, their wives and the Widow Bartley.

Three of them—Reverend Hobson, Doctor Robinson, and Lawyer Bell—had left town on business. But the others would stay. They shook hands with the king and thanked him. Then they shook hands with the duke but didn't say anything, just smiled and bobbed their heads like a lot of sapheads. The duke made signs with his hands.

Then Mary Jane fetched the letter that Peter had left for Harvey and handed it to the king. He read it out loud and cried over it. The letter willed the home and three thousand in gold to the girls. Other houses and land—worth about seven thousand—and three thousand in gold went to Harvey and William. The letter told where the six thousand cash was hid down cellar.

So the king said he and his brother William would go and fetch it up. He told me to come along with a candle. They found the bag and emptied the gold out on the floor. It was a lovely sight. My, how the king's eyes did shine! They pawed through the coins, sifted them through their fingers, and let them jingle down on the floor. Next, they must count it. It added up four hundred and fifteen dollars short.

"Dern him, I wonder what he done with that four hundred and fifteen dollars."

They looked all around for it. Then the duke said:

"Maybe he made a mistake. Let it go and keep still about it. We can spare it."

"Oh, shucks, yes; we can *spare* it. But the *count* is what I'm thinking about. We want to be square and above board here, you know. We want to lug this money upstairs and count it before everybody. The dead man said there was six thousand, and we don't want to come up short."

"Hold on," said the duke. "Let's make up the difference." And he began to haul money out of his pocket.

"A good idea, duke. You *have* got a rattlin' clever head on you." And *he* began to haul out money.

It 'most busted them, but they made up the six thousand. We went upstairs, and everybody gathered around the table while the king counted the money and stacked it up. Everybody looked hungry at it. Then the king raked it all into the bag again, and swelled himself up for a speech. A big iron-jawed man had worked himself in from outside. He stood looking and listening but not saying anything.

The king was saying: "You here are the close friends of brother Peter. That is why you are invited this evening. But tomorrow we want *all* to come—everybody. Peter liked everybody, and it is fittin' that his funeral orgies be public." He went mooning on and on, liking to hear himself talk. He kept talking about the funeral "orgies" till the duke couldn't stand it any longer. He wrote on a scrap of paper, *"Obsequies,* you old fool," and handed it to the king. The king read the note, put it in his pocket and said:

"Poor William! Deaf and dumb as he is, his heart is always right. He has asked me in this note to invite everybody to the funeral—just what I was doing." Then he went weaving along in his speech, and spoke again of the funeral "orgies." This time he added:

"I say *orgies* because that is the right word in England. *Obsequies* is the common word here, but it ain't used in England now. Funeral *orgies* is more exact; it means an open or public funeral."

Well, the iron-jawed man laughed right in his face. Everybody was shocked.

"Why, Doctor Robinson," said Abner Shackleford, "didn't you hear the news? This is Harvey Wilks."

The king smiled and shoved out his hand to Doctor Robinson.

"Keep your hands off me!" said the doctor. "*You* talk like an Englishman, *don't* you! The worst imitation I ever heard. *You* Peter Wilks's brother! You are a fraud!"

They crowded around the doctor, and tried to quiet him down, and told him how Harvey had called them all by name, and how he showed in forty ways that he *was* Harvey. But it was no use. The doctor stormed right along. Then he turned to the girls and said:

"I warn you to turn your backs on this ignorant tramp. He comes here with a lot of facts he picked up somewhere, and you take that for proof he is Harvey Wilks. You have all helped to fool yourselves. Now listen to me: Turn this pitiful rascal out—I *beg* you to do it. Will you?"

Mary Jane straightened up and said: *"This* is my answer." She picked up the bag of money and put it in the king's hands. "Take our part of this six thousand dollars and invest it for us. Don't give us a receipt for it."

Everybody clapped and stomped on the floor, while the king held his head high and smiled proud. The doctor said:

"All right. But the time is coming when you will be sick whenever you think of this day."

"When they get sick they can send for you, doctor," the king called after the doctor as he went out the door.

Everybody laughed; they said that was a prime good hit.

20 Dead Peter Has His Gold

That night we had a big supper. I stood behind the king's chair and waited on him, and the servants waited on the rest.

After supper the king asked Mary Jane about sleeping rooms. She said Uncle William could have the spare room, and she would give her own room to Uncle Harvey, for it was a bigger room. She would sleep on a cot in the room with her sisters. Up garret was a little cubby with a pallet in it. The king said this would do for his valley*—meaning me.

I lit out for bed as soon as I had supper. When I got by myself I went to thinking. I had to save that money for the girls. There was only one way to do it. I had to steal the money somehow. Steal it and hide it. Then by and by when I was away down the river, write a letter to tell Mary Jane where it was. But I must steal it tonight. It wasn't likely that the doctor had let up on them, and if he scared them bad enough they might run away with the money before day.

Upstairs the hall was dark, but I found the duke's room and started to paw around it. Then I thought the king wouldn't be likely to let that money out of

* Valet, a man servant.

his hands. So I went to his room and began to paw around. About that time I heard them coming up the stairs, and I skipped behind a curtain. They walked in and shut the door. The king said:

"Well, what is it? Cut it short. We ought to be down there whoopin' up the mourning instead of up here giving them a chance to talk it over."

"I tell you I ain't easy. That doctor worries me. We better glide out of here before morning and be satisfied with what we got."

The king rips out and says, "What! March off like a couple of fools and leave eight or nine thousand dollars in property—all good salable stuff!"

The duke grumbled, said six thousand cash was enough, said it was blamed foolishness to stay, with that doctor hanging over them. But the king said:

"Curse the doctor! What do we care for him? Haven't we got all the fools in town on our side? And ain't that big enough majority in any town?"

Then the duke said, "I don't think we put that money in a good place."

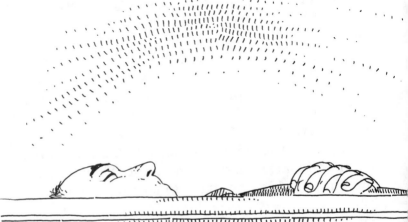

But the king said it was all right, because a servant only makes up the feather bed, and won't turn over the straw tick more than twice a year.

I had the bag of money out of there before they could get downstairs, and groped up to my cubby. I judged I had better hide the money outside the house. When they missed it, they would give the house a good ransacking. I waited until I heard the king and the duke come up, and everything was still downstairs. Then I crept up to their doors and listened. I could hear them snoring.

I went back for the bag of money and crept downstairs. The men watching the corpse had gone to sleep in their chairs. I tiptoed on through to the front door. It was locked, and the key wasn't there. Just then I thought I heard somebody coming down the stairs. I took a swift look around, and the only place I saw to hide the bag of money was in the coffin. I shoved the lid back and tucked the bag away down beyond where the hands crossed. The hands felt so cold it made me creep, and I got out of there as fast

as I could. When I got back to my bed I thought, "When we get down the river a hundred miles or so I'll write back to Mary Jane, and she can dig him up and get the money."

Next morning when I went downstairs, the parlor was shut up, and the watchers had gone. Nobody was around but the family and the Widow Bartley and our own tribe. I watched their faces to see if they had missed the money. But I couldn't tell.

Toward the middle of the day the undertaker came with his man. They set the coffin in the middle of the room and put rows of chairs all around the walls. Then the people flocked in. For half an hour they filed around slow, in single rank, and looked down on the dead man's face. It was all very still and solemn. The girls and the king and the duke bent their heads, and sobbed in their handkerchiefs.

Then the undertaker slid around with his soft soothing ways, getting people seated. He made no more noise than a cat, as he moved people around, squeezed in late comers, and opened up passage ways, doing it with nods and signs made with his black gloved hands. He was the softest, glidingest man I ever saw. And there was no more smile to him than there is to a ham.

When everything was ready, the Reverend Hobson got up to talk, slow and solemn. Right after he opened up, the most outrageous row busted out in the cellar. It was only one dog, but he made a powerful racket, and kept it up. The parson had to stop. He just stood over the coffin and waited. The undertaker made a sign to him as much as to say, "Don't you worry—just depend on me." Then he went gliding along the wall behind the rows of chairs, and when he had gone around two sides of the room, he went through the door. In about two minutes we heard a whack, and the dog finished up with a howl. Then everything was dead still, and the parson took up his solemn talk where he left off.

In a minute or two here comes the undertaker back, gliding along the walls again. He shaded his mouth with his hands and stretched his neck out toward the preacher and said in a coarse whisper, *"He had a rat!"* Naturally the people had wanted to know. Little services like that don't cost anything and make a man liked.

The funeral was very good, but p'ison* long and tiresome. At last the job was through, and the undertaker sneaked up on the coffin with his screw-driver. I was in a sweat, and watched him pretty keen. But he didn't meddle, just slid the lid along and screwed it down.

So there I was! I didn't know whether the money was in there or not. How was I to know whether to write Mary Jane? Suppose she dug him up and didn't find anything. What would she think of me? Blame it, I said to myself, I wish to goodness I had let it alone. Dad fetch the whole business!

They buried him, and we went back home, and I went to watching faces. I couldn't rest easy. But the faces didn't tell me anything.

That evening the king visited around and sweetened everybody up and made himself ever so friendly. He let it be known that his church in England was in a sweat for him to come back, so he must settle the estate right away and leave for England. He was very sorry he was so pushed, he wished he could stay longer, but it couldn't be done. He said of course he and William would take the

* poison.

girls back to England with them. That pleased the girls so they clean forgot they ever had a sorrow and told him to sell out as quick as he wanted to.

Well, blamed if the king didn't bill the house and the slaves and all the property for auction right off—sale two days after the funeral, but anybody could buy beforehand if he wanted to. Next day along about noon a couple of slave-traders come along. The king sold them the slaves cheap, for three-day draft.* Two sons were sold up the river to Memphis, and their mother down the river to Orleans.

The poor girls cried and said they hadn't dreamed of seeing the family separated or sold away from that town. I can't get it out of my memory, the sight of the poor miserable girls and the slaves hanging around each other's neck and crying. I would have busted out and told on our gang if I hadn't thought the sale was no account and the slaves would be back in a week or two.

The thing made a big stir in the town, too. A good many people came out flat-footed and said it was wrong to separate the mother and children that way. It injured the frauds some, but that old fool king bulled right along, in spite of all the duke could do. I tell you the duke was powerful uneasy.

About daylight the morning of the auction the king and the duke climbed up to my garret and waked me up. I saw by their look that there was trouble. The king said:

"Have you been in my room?"

"No," I said.

"Have you seen anybody go in there?"

I studied a while, and saw my chance. "Well, I

---

* To be paid for in three days.

saw the slaves that you sold go in there several times."

"What, *all* of them?"

"I don't think I ever saw them all come *out* at once, except one time. It was the day of the funeral. They tiptoed out. I saw they had shoved in there to do up your room, thinking you out, but found you in there asleep. At least, they seemed to be trying to get away without waking you."

"Great guns!" said the king.

They both stood there thinking, and looking pretty sick and silly. The duke said:

"They let on to be *sorry* they had to leave. Oh, yes, mighty sorry! And to think you sold them for a song."

"Is something gone wrong?" I said, kind of timid-like.

The king whirled on me and ripped out, "None of your business. You keep your head shut, and mind your own affairs. Long as you are in this town, don't forget *that*—you hear?" Then he said to the duke, "We got to swallow it and say nothing."

As they started downstairs the duke said with a little raspy chuckle, "Quick sale and small profit! It *was* good business—yes. If you had listened to me, they would be here yet, and we *wouldn't.*"

The king snarled around on him and sassed back, and then lit into *me* again. Why hadn't I come and told him I had seen them come sneaking out of his room—any fool would know they were up to something.

They went off a-jawin', and I felt glad I had worked it off onto the slaves, and yet hadn't done them any harm by it.

21 *The King Overreaches Himself*

I got up and started downstairs. The girls' room was open as I passed, and I saw Mary Jane in there. She'd been packing a trunk, getting ready to go to England. But she had stopped with a folded gown in her lap and had her face in her hands crying. I went in and asked her what was the matter.

It was about the slaves—just as I expected. She said the beautiful trip to England was spoiled for her. She could never be happy again, knowing the mother and two sons would never see each other again.

"But they *will*—inside of two weeks—and I *know* it!" It was out before I could think!

She hugged me for joy and asked how I could know that. I saw I had said too much and was in a tight place. It looked like here was a case where truth would be better and *safer* than a lie. Anyway I thought, I'd chance it. Then I said:

"Don't you holler, just keep still and take it like a man. These men are not your uncles, but a couple of frauds—regular dead-beats."

It jolted her hard. But I went right on and told her every blame thing, from when we first met that young fool going up to the steamboat, clear through to where she flung herself into her "uncle's" arms at the front door and kissed him. Her eyes blazed brighter and brighter.

"Come, don't waste a minute. We'll have them tarred and feathered and flung into the river!"

"But they are a rough gang, these two frauds. And I have to travel with them a while longer, whether I want to or not. I'd rather not tell you why. If you give them away, the town would get me out of their claws, and *I* would be all right. But there's another person, who would be in big trouble."

"Tell me what to do. Whatever you say I'll do!"

Then I saw how maybe I could get rid of the frauds—get them jailed here, and then leave. But I didn't want to run the raft in the daytime—the plan couldn't be worked till late tonight. I said:

"Is there any place out of town a little ways, where you could go and stay a while?"

"Yes; Mr. Lothrop's. Why?"

"You go there and keep out of sight till about eleven o'clock tonight. You're not one of these leather-face people—you can't face your uncles when they come to kiss you good morning without—"

"Don't—don't. I'll go before breakfast. And leave my sisters with them?"

"The frauds might suspect something if all of you left. You go right along. I'll tell your sisters you went away for a little rest and change, and you'll be back tonight. Just let the auction go right along and don't worry. They won't be able to collect the money for everything today and they won't leave till they get it all. If I haven't turned up by eleven o'clock tonight, it means I'm gone out of the way, and safe. Then you go out and spread the news in town about these frauds and get them jailed."

"Good," she said. "I'll do it."

"I'll tell you how to prove these uncles are frauds. Give me a pencil and a piece of paper." I wrote on the paper, *Royal Nonesuch, Bricksville.* "There, keep that, and when the court wants to find out about these two frauds, send up to Bricksville and tell the people there that you have the men that played the *Royal Nonesuch,* and need some witnesses. The whole town will be down here before you can wink. Now there's one more thing—the bag of money."

"Well, they've got that. It makes me feel pretty silly to think *how* they got it."

"No, they haven't got it. I stole it from them to give back to you. I know where I hid it, but I'm not sure it's there anymore."

"Where did you hide it?"

I hated to set her to thinking about her sorrow again. And I couldn't get my mouth to tell her that the corpse was in his coffin with that bag of money on his stomach. So I said, "I'd rather not *tell* you where I put it. But I'll write it on a piece of paper. You can read it later. Will that do?"

"Oh, yes."

"So I wrote: *I put it in the coffin.* Then I folded the paper and handed it to her.

She shook my hand hard and said, "Good-bye. I am going to do just as you told me. If I don't see you again, I won't ever forget you. And I will pray for you, too." And she was gone.

Pray for me! She might have taken a job nearer her size, but I bet she tried, just the same. She was just that kind. I haven't ever seen her since, but I've thought of her a million times, and of her saying she would pray for me. If I thought it would ever do any good for *me* to pray for *her,* blamed if I wouldn't do it or bust.

Well, Mary Jane lit out the back way. Nobody saw her go. Then I went to find Susan and Joanna, and said:

"What is the name of the family over on the other side of the river that you all go to see sometimes?"

"There are several, but we go to the Proctors mainly."

"That was the name," I said. "I almost forgot it. Well, Miss Mary Jane said to tell you she's gone over there in a dreadful hurry—one of them is sick."

"Which one? Hannah?"

"Yes, Hannah is the very one."

"What's the matter with her?"

"Mumps. They had to watch her all night."

"Mumps, your granny. They don't watch people with mumps."

"But this is mixed up with some other things—measles, whooping-cough, janders, brain-fever."

"My land! What in the nation do they call it mumps for?"

"Because that was what it started with."

"Suppose a body stumped his toe and took poison and fell down a well and broke his neck and busted his brains out. If something asked you what killed him, would you say, 'Why, he stumped his toe'?"

"Is it catching?" asked the other sister.

"Is a *harrow* catching? If one tooth won't catch you, another one will."

"Well, I'll go to Uncle Harvey and—"

"Now just look at it a minute. Your Uncle Harvey is a preacher, and would a preacher deceive a steamboat clerk so as to get Miss Mary Jane aboard? You know he wouldn't. He'd say, 'My niece has been exposed to mumps, and we must wait three months before we can start to England.'"

"But we ought to tell Uncle Harvey she has gone out for a while, so he won't be uneasy about her."

"Yes, she wanted you to do that. She said, 'Tell Uncle Harvey I have gone over the river to see—What *is* the name of that rich family over there?"

"You must mean the Apthorps."

"Yes. She said to say she had run over to ask the Apthorps to come to the auction and buy this house. She'll be home by morning, anyway."

"All right," they said, and went off to give their Uncle Harvey the message.

Everything was all right now. I judged Tom Sawyer couldn't have done it any neater himself, though of course he would have put more style into it.

They held the auction in the public square that afternoon late. By and by the thing dragged through, and everything was sold. Everything but a little old lot in the graveyard. I never saw such a giraffe as the king for wanting to swallow everything. While the auctioneer was working off the graveyard lot, up comes a crowd, whooping and laughing and yelling out:

"Here is another set of heirs to old Peter Wilks! Pay your money and take your choice!"

They had with them a very nice-looking old gentleman and a nice-looking younger one, with his right arm in a sling. My soul, how the people yelled and laughed, and kept it up. But I didn't see any joke about it, and I reckoned the duke and the king would turn pale. But nothing of the kind. The duke never let on that he could hear a word. As for the king, he just gazed down sorrowful on the new comers, as if it caused him stomach-ache in his very heart to know such frauds could be.

The old gentleman that had just come looked puzzled to death. Pretty soon he began to speak, and he *did* pronounce like an Englishman.

"Gentlemen, I am Peter Wilks's brother Harvey, and this is his brother William, who can't hear or speak. We have had misfortunes. He broke his arm,

and our baggage was put off the boat by mistake, at a town above here, last night. But we are who we say we are, and in a day or two, when I get the baggage, I can prove it. Until then, I'll go to the hotel and wait."

The king laughed and bawled out: "Very likely story! Lost their baggage! Ha, ha, ha!"

Everybody laughed except three or four. One of these was that doctor. Another was a sharp-looking gentleman with a carpet bag. He had just come off the steamboat. He was Levi Bell, the lawyer. Another was a big rough husky that had come along and was listening to the king now.

"Say," he said to the king, "if you are Harvey Wilks, when did you come to this town?"

"The day before the funeral, friend," said the king.

"How did you come?"

"On the *Susan Powell* from Cincinnati."

"I live up at the point, and I saw you there that day. You come in a canoe with a boy."

The doctor spoke up: "Would you know that boy again if you saw him, Hines?"

"I reckon I would, but I don't know. Why, yonder he is now." He pointed to me.

The doctor said, "Neighbors, I don't know anything about the new couple. But if *these* two are not frauds" (he pointed to the king and the duke) "I'm an idiot. I think our duty is to look into this thing. Come along, Hines. Come along, the rest of you. We'll take these fellows to the tavern, and I reckon we'll find out *something* before we get through."

We all started. It was about sundown. The doctor led me along by the hand. He was kind enough, but he never let go my hand.

22   *I Light Out in the Storm*

We all got in a big room in the tavern, and they lit up some candles. First the doctor said:

"I don't wish to be too hard on these two men, but *I* think they are frauds. These other two may be in their gang. If they *are* frauds we don't want them to get away with the property that Peter Wilks left. If they are all right, they won't object to sending for that bag of gold and letting us hold it till they *prove* they are all right."

Everybody agreed, so I judged our gang was in a tight place. But the king only looked sorrowful and said:

"Gentlemen, I wish the money was here, but alas it ain't."

"Where is it then?"

"The slaves stole it, and I sold them before I had missed the money. My servant here" (meaning me) "can tell you about it."

The doctor and several others said "Shucks!" One man asked me if I saw them steal it. I said no, but I saw them sneaking out of the room where it was kept. The doctor whirled on me and said:

"Are *you* English, too?"

I said yes. They all laughed and said "Stuff!" Then they had me up to tell what I knew about it. The king sent me a left-handed look out of the corner of his eye. I saw I had better talk on the right side.

I began to tell about England and all the English Wilkses. I didn't get far before Levi Bell said:

"You can stop, my boy. I wouldn't strain myself. I reckon you are not used to lying, you do it so poor."

The king reached out his hand to the lawyer and said: "Is this my poor dead brother's old friend, Levi Bell? He wrote so often about you."

The lawyer shook his hand and looked pleased. They talked right along a while. Then the lawyer took the king to one side and talked low. At last the lawyer spoke up and said:

"That will fix it. I'll take the order and send it along with your brother's order."

They got paper and pen, and the king twisted his head to one side and scrawled off something. Then the lawyer handed the pen to the duke—and for the first time the duke looked sick. But he took the pen and wrote. Then the lawyer turned to the new old gentleman and said:

"You and your brother please write a line or two and sign your names."

The old gentleman wrote, but nobody could read it. Then the lawyer snaked some old letters out of his pocket and looked at them, and looked at the writing done by the king and the duke. He said:

"These old letters are from Harvey Wilks. Anybody can see that the handwriting of these two men is not that of Harvey Wilks."

The king and the duke looked sold and foolish to see how the lawyer had tricked them. Lawyer Bell went on speaking:

"But what beats *me* is that this old gentleman's handwriting is not Harvey Wilks's, either. Fact is, the scratching he does is hardly *writing*. I can't read a word of it."

The new old gentleman said: "Let me explain. My handwriting is so poor nobody can read it but my brother there. So he copies for me. It is *his* handwriting you have there in the old letters, not mine."

"Well!" said the lawyer, "this *is* a state of things. If you will get him to write a line or two we can compare—"

"He *can't* write with his left hand," said the old gentleman.

"Well, well, well!" said the lawyer. "I thought I had the problem solved, but my plan has gone to grass. Anyway, *one* thing is proved—*this* is not Harvey Wilks," and he nodded toward the king.

Well, that mule-headed old fool wouldn't give in *then.* He said it was no fair test. He warmed up and went warbling along till he was beginning to believe *himself.* Pretty soon the new gentleman broke in:

"I have thought of something. Is there anybody here that helped to lay out my brother Peter Wilks for burying?"

"Yes," said somebody. "Me and Ab Turner did. We are both here."

The old gentleman turned to the king and said, "Maybe you can tell me what was tattooed on his breast?"

He whitened a little. I said to myself, *"Now* he will throw up the sponge." Well, he didn't. I never saw anything like that old blister for clean out-and-out cheek. I reckon he thought he would keep the thing up till he tired the people and he could break loose and get away.

"Yes, sir," he said, "I can tell you what was tattooed on his breast. A blue arrow—small. If you didn't look close, you couldn't see it."

Both of the men spoke up. "We didn't see such a mark."

"Good," said the old gentleman. "Now I will tell you what you *did* see on his breast. Three small letters, P B W. Come, now, isn't that what you saw?"

"No, we didn't. We didn't see any marks at all."

Everybody began whooping at once and singing out: "The whole gang is a fraud! Duck 'em! Drown 'em! Ride 'em on a rail!"

But the lawyer said, "There is one way yet. Let's go dig up the corpse and look."

"Hooray!" they all shouted. "And if we don't find the marks, lynch the whole gang!"

I *was* scared now. But there was no getting away. They gripped us all and marched us along to the graveyard. Hines hung on to my wrist so tight it hurt. We swarmed along the road like wild cats. It was night now, about nine o'clock. To make it more scary, the sky was clouding up, the lightning beginning to wink and flitter, and the wind to shiver in the leaves.

The crowd swarmed into the graveyard and washed over it like an overflow. When they got to the grave, they found they had about a hundred times as many shovels as they needed, but nobody had thought to bring a lantern. They sent a man to the nearest house, half a mile off, to borrow one, and sailed in to digging by the lightning flickers. The rain started, and the wind swished along, and the lightning got brisker, and the thunder boomed.

At last they got out the coffin and began to unscrew the lid. Then such crowding and shouldering and shoving to get a sight, you never did see. In the dark that way, it was awful. All of a sudden the lightning let go a perfect sluice of white glare, and somebody sung out:

"By the living jingo, here's the bag of gold on his breast!"

Hines let out a whoop like everybody else, dropped my wrist and surged up to bust his way in for a look. The way I lit out and shinned for the road in the dark nobody can tell. I had the road all to myself, and I fairly flew through the solid dark and the now-and-then glares of lightning. The rain was buzzing, and the wind was thrashing, and the thunder was splitting. Sure as you are born I did clip it along! When I struck the town nobody was out in the storm, so I humped it along straight through the main street. When I got near our house, I aimed my eye and set it. No light there; the house all dark—which made me feel sorry and kind of hurt, I didn't know why. But at last, just as I was sailing by, *flash* comes the light in Mary Jane's window, and my heart swelled up sudden, like to bust. The same second the house and all was behind me in the dark, and wasn't ever going to be before me again in this world. She *was* the best girl I ever did see, and had the most sand.

I got down to the river and looked sharp for a boat to borrow. The first one the lightning showed me I snatched and shoved off. The towhead was out there in the middle of the river, but I didn't lose any time. When I got to the raft I was so fagged I would have stretched out to blow and gasp if I could afforded it. But just the minute I sprung aboard I yelled out:

"Come on, Jim, set her loose! Glory be to goodness, we're shut of them! Cut loose and let her slide!"

In two seconds we went sliding down the river. It *did* seem good to be free again, all by ourselves, on the big river. I had to skip around and jump up and crack my heels a few times. But about the third crack I heard a sound. I held my breath and listened. Sure enough, when the next flash of lightning busted out over the water, here they come—and just laying to their oars and making their skiff hum! It was the king and the duke. I wilted right down. It was all I could do to keep from crying.

When they got aboard, the king went for me and shook me by the collar.

"Trying to give us the slip, you pup! Tired of our company, hey? Tell me what was your idea of running away, or I will shake the insides out of you!"

"It didn't seem any good for me to stay—I couldn't do anything, and I didn't want to be hung, if I could get away."

"Oh yes, a likely story," and he shook me up again, and said he reckoned he would drown me. But the duke said:

"Let go that boy, you old idiot! Did *you* do any different? Did you inquire around for *him* when you got loose? I don't remember it."

So the king let go of me, and commenced to cuss that town and everybody in it. But the duke said:

"You better give yourself a good cussing. You haven't done a thing from the start, that had any sense in it—except to come out so cheeky for that blue-arrow mark. That trick took 'em to the grave-yard. If the fools hadn't found the gold and got so excited they let go all holds, we would have been strung up. How *did* that bag of gold get in there?"

They kept still a minute—thinking. Then the king said, kind of absent-minded:

"And *I* thought the servants stole it!"

"Yes," said the duke, kind of slow and sarcastic. "You *did* think that."

The king ruffled up and said, "Look here, Bilgewater, what are you referring to?"

"When it comes to that, maybe you'll let me ask what are *you* referring to?"

"Shucks!" said the king, very sarcastic. "Maybe you walked in your sleep and didn't know when you put it there."

The duke bristled up and said, "Oh, let up on this cussed nonsense. Do you think you can fool me? I know who hid that money in the coffin."

"*Yes,* sir! You *do* know, because you put it there yourself!"

"It's a lie!" Then the duke went for him, till the king sung out:

"Take your hands off—let go my throat—I take it all back! Let go!"

"Not till you own up that you hid that money in the coffin intending to give me the slip and go back and dig it up for yourself!"

The king began to gurgle, and then he gasped out, " 'Nough! I own up!"

The duke took his hands off and said, "If you ever deny it again I'll drown you, I never saw such an old ostrich for wanting to gobble everything. And now what have you got for it? They have all their money back, and all ours too! Get out of my sight!"

The king sneaked into the wigwam and took to his bottle. Before long the duke tackled *his* bottle. In half an hour they got thick as thieves again, and went off snoring in each other's arms.

23 *You Can't Pray a Lie*

We didn't dare stop again at any town for days and days. We kept right along down the river. We had got down south now, in the warm weather, and a long way from home. We began to come to trees with Spanish moss on them, hanging down from the limbs like long, gray beards. It made the woods look solemn and dismal.

Then the duke and the king thought they would be safe to begin to work the villages again. First they had a lecture on temperance, but didn't make enough to get drunk on. In another village they started a dancing school, but they didn't know any more about how to dance than a kangaroo does. Other times they tackled telling fortunes, and doctoring, and preaching. But they didn't have any luck. At last they got just about dead broke, and loafed around the raft as she floated along, never saying anything for half a day at a time, and dreadful blue and desperate.

Then they took a change and began to lay their heads together in the wigwam, talking low for hours at a time. Jim got uneasy, and so did I. We didn't like the look of it. We judged they would think up some deviltry worse than ever. They might be planning to break into a house or store, or make counterfeit money, or something. We were pretty scared. We

147

agreed that if we ever got the least chance we would clear out and leave them behind.

Early one morning we hid the raft in a good safe place, about two miles below a shabby little village named Pikeville. The king went ashore and told us all to stay hid while he went up to town and smelt around to see if anybody there had got wind of the *Royal Nonesuch.*

"Yes, you are going to hunt a house to rob," I said to myself. "And when you get through robbing it, you will wonder what has become of me and Jim and the raft."

He said if he didn't get back by midday the duke would know it was all right, and we could come along.

So we stayed behind. The duke fretted around and was in a mighty sour way. He scolded us for everything; we couldn't seem to do anything right. Something was brewing sure.

I was good and glad when midday passed and no king. We could have a change anyway. The duke went up to the village and took me with him. We hunted around for the king, and by and by we found him, so tight he couldn't walk. The duke abused him for an old fool, and the king sassed right back. The minute they were fairly at it, I lit out. I shook the reefs out of my hind legs and spun down the river road like a deer.

I got back to the raft all out of breath but loaded up with joy. I sung out:

"Set her loose, Jim. We are all right now!"

But there was no answer. Jim was gone! I set up a shout and went this way and that in the woods, whooping and screeching. It was no use—old Jim was gone. Then I cried for a while. But pretty soon

I started up the road, trying to think what I had better do. I met a boy and asked him if he had seen a runaway slave and he said:

"Yes, down at Silas Phelps's place, two miles below here. Are you looking for him?"

I said, "You bet I am not! I met him an hour or two ago and he said if I hollered he would cut my livers out—and told me to stay where I was, and I did. Been there ever since, afraid to come out."

"Well," he said, "you needn't be afraid now. They've caught him. There was a two hundred dollar reward."

"That was a lot of money. Who nailed him?"

"An old fellow—a stranger. He sold out his chance in the reward for forty dollars. He said he had to go on up the river, and couldn't wait to collect the whole two hundred dollars."

"But maybe his chance is not worth more than that, if he can sell it so cheap. Maybe there's something not straight about it."

"But it is straight—straight as a string. I saw the handbill myself. It described him to a dot, and told the plantation he run away from, down below New Orleans."

I went back to the raft and wore my head sore trying to think my way out of trouble. To think the two old frauds would have the heart to serve Jim such a mean trick, after all we had done for them! To think they would sell him into slavery again, and among strangers, for forty dirty dollars!

Once I thought I'd write a letter to Tom Sawyer and tell him to let Miss Watson know where Jim was. It would be better for Jim to be a slave at home, where his family was, as long as he had to be a slave. But, then, Miss Watson would be sure to sell him down the river, because he had run away. And if she didn't, everybody just naturally despises an ungrateful slave. And they would make Jim feel it all the time, ornery and disgraced. And then think of *me!* It would get around that Huck Finn helped a slave run away.

At last it hit me all of a sudden. This was the hand of Providence slapping me in the face for my wickedness. I was being watched up there in heaven all the time I was stealing a poor old woman's slave. The more I thought, the more my conscience went to grinding me, and the more wicked and low-down I got to feeling. I made up my mind to pray and see if I couldn't be better. So I kneeled down, but the words wouldn't come. Why? It was because my heart wasn't right; I wasn't being square; I was playing double. I was pretending to give up sin, but I was holding on to the biggest sin of all. I was trying to make my mouth *say* I would do the right thing, and write to Jim's owner and tell where he was, but it was a lie. You can't pray a lie—I found that out.

So I was full of trouble, and didn't know what to do. At last I had an idea. I said, I'll go and write the letter—and *then* see if I can pray. So I got a piece of paper and a pencil, all glad and excited, and set down and wrote:

> Miss Watson your runaway slave Jim is down here two mile below Pikesville and Mr. Phelps has got him and he will give him up for reward if you send.
>
> HUCK FINN

I felt good and all washed clean of sin for the first time in my life, and I knew I could pray now.

But then I kept thinking over our trip down the river, floating along, talking and singing and laughing. I thought how good Jim was to me, sometimes standing my watch so I could go on sleeping, and how glad he was when I turned up, out of the fog, how he would always call me honey and pet me, and do everything he could for me.

I took up the letter, and held it in my hand. I was trembling, because I'd got to decide, forever, betwixt two things, and I knew it. I studied a minute, sort of holding my breath, and then said to myself:

"All right, then, I'll *go* to hell"—and tore it up.

It was awful thoughts, and awful words, but they were said. And I let them stay said. I would take up wickedness again, which was in my line, being brought up to it, and the other wasn't. And for a starter, I would go and steal Jim out of slavery again. And if I could think up anything worse, I would do that too. As long as I was in sin, and in for good, I might as well go the whole hog.

Then I set to thinking and at last fixed up a plan that suited me. So I took the bearings of a woody island that was down the river a piece, and as soon as it was fairly dark I crept out with my raft and went for it. I hid the raft, and turned in and slept the night through. Next morning I got up before it was light, had my breakfast, tied up some things in a bundle, and took the canoe and went for the shore. I landed below where I judged Phelps's place was, and hid my bundle in the woods. Then I filled up the canoe with water and loaded rocks into her, and sunk her where I could find her again later when I wanted her.

Then I struck up the road that went by a little steam-sawmill on the bank. When I passed the mill

I saw a sign on it, "Phelps's Sawmill." A farmhouse was two or three hundred yards farther along. I kept my eyes peeled, but didn't see anybody around, though it was good daylight now. But I didn't want to see anybody just yet. I only wanted to get the lay of the land. I planned to turn up to that farmhouse as coming from the village, not from below it. So I just took a look, then shoved along, straight for the town.

Well, the very first man I saw when I got there was the duke. He was sticking up a bill for the *Royal Nonesuch*—three-night performance. I was right on him before I could duck. He looked surprised and said:

"Hel-lo! Where did *you* come from?" Then he said, kind of glad and eager, "Where is the raft? Got her in a good place?"

I said, "Why, I was going to ask you that."

Then he didn't look so joyful, and said, "What was your idea for asking *me?*"

"Well, when I saw the king yesterday, I thought it would be hours before he would be sober enough for you to get him back to the raft. So I went loafing around town to put in the time. A man offered me ten cents to help him row a skiff over the river to bring back a sheep. So I went along. But the sheep broke away when we tried to get him on the boat, and we had to chase him all over the country. It was dark before we caught him and got back on this side of the river. I started down for the raft, and when I got there it was gone. I slept in the woods all night. But what *did* become of the raft and Jim—poor Jim!"

"Blamed if I know what happened to the raft. That old fool had made a trade and got forty dollars.

When we found him he had gambled away every cent of it but what he had spent for whiskey. When I got him back to the river the raft was gone. We said, 'That little rascal stole the raft and left us.' "

"I wouldn't go leave my only slave, would I?"

"Well, the raft was gone, and we flat broke. There was nothing to do but try the *Royal Nonesuch* again. I'm dry as a powder-horn. Where is that ten cents? Give it here."

I had some money but didn't want him to know. So when I let him have the ten cents, I begged him to spend it for something to eat and to give me some of it, because I hadn't had anything to eat since yesterday. He didn't answer. The next minute he whirled on me and said:

"Do you reckon that slave would blow on us? We would skin him if he did!"

"How can he blow? Hasn't he run off?"

"No! That old fool sold him for forty dollars, and never divided with me, and the money is gone."

"Sold him?" I said and began to cry. "Why, he was *my* slave."

"Well, your slave is gone—so dry up your blubbering. Look here—do you think *you* would venture to blow on us? Why, if you *dared* to blow on us—"

He stopped, but I never saw the duke look so ugly out of his eyes. I went on crying and said:

"I don't want to blow on anybody. I don't have time, anyhow. I got to go find him."

He looked bothered, and stood there with his bills fluttering on his arm, thinking and wrinkling up his forehead. At last he said:

"I'll tell you something. We got to be here three days. If you promise you won't blow and won't let him blow, I'll tell you where to find him."

I promised, and he said:

"A farmer by the name of Silas Ph—" and then he stopped.

I saw he had started to tell me the truth. When he stopped and began to study, I reckoned he was changing his mind. And so he was. He wouldn't trust me. And he wanted to get me out of the way for three days.

"The man that bought him is named Abram Foster—Abram G. Foster. He lives forty miles back in the country, on the road to Lafayette."

"All right," I said, "I can walk it in three days. I'll start this very afternoon."

"No you won't, you'll start now. And don't you do any gabbling by the way. Just keep a tight tongue in your head and move right along, and then you won't get into trouble with *us*. Do you hear? You can tell Mr. Foster whatever you want to. Maybe you can get him to believe that Jim *is* your slave—some idiots don't ask for papers—at least I've heard there's such down South here. And when you tell him the handbill offering the reward is bogus, maybe he'll believe you when you explain to him why we got out the handbill offering the reward. Go along now, and tell him anything you want to, but don't work your jaw any *between* here and there."

I left and struck for the back country. I didn't look around, but I felt that he was watching me. I went straight out in the country as much as a mile before I stopped. Then I doubled back through the woods toward Phelps's. I reckoned I had better start in on my plan right off, because I wanted to stop Jim's mouth till these fellows could get away. I didn't want any trouble with them. All I wanted was to be entirely rid of them.

24 *I Have a New Name*

When I got to the Phelps's place, everything was still and Sunday-like. The hands had gone to the fields. It was hot and sunshiny, and there was that faint droning of flies that sounds so lonesome you feel like everybody is dead and gone.

The place was a little one-horse cotton plantation, looking like every other one of its kind. A rail fence around a two-acre yard, bare and smooth except for some sickly grass patches. A big double log house for the white folks. A log kitchen joined to it by a broad, roofed passage. A smoke house back of the kitchen. A row of slave cabins. One little hut all by itself away down against the back fence. Some outbuilding down a piece on the other side. A bench by the kitchen door with a bucket of water and a gourd. Hound asleep there in the sun, more hounds asleep round about. About three shade trees off in a corner. Some currant bushes and gooseberry bushes by the fence. Outside the fence a garden and a watermelon patch. Then the cotton fields, and after the fields the woods.

When I got near the house, first one hound and then another got up and went for me. I stopped and stood still. In a quarter of a minute I was the hub of a wheel—spokes made of fifteen dogs barking and howling, and more coming. You could see them all sailing over fences and around corners from everywhere.

A cook tore out of the kitchen with a rolling pin in her hand, singing out: "Begone! *You* Tige! You Spot! begone sah!" She fetched first one and then another of them a clip and sent them howling away, and the rest followed. The next second half of them trotted back, wagging their tails around me and making friends. There's no harm in a hound.

Behind the woman came a little girl and two little boys with nothing on but tow-linen shirts. They hung on to their mother's gown and peeped out from behind her, very bashful.

And then a white woman comes running bare-headed, with her little children acting the same as the other little children. She was smiling all over.

"It's *you*, at last—ain't it?"

I out with a "Yes'm" before I thought.

She grabbed me and hugged me tight while tears rolled down her face.

"You don't look much like your mother," she said. "But I'm so glad to see you. Children, it's your cousin Tom! Tell him howdy!"

But they ducked their heads and put their fingers in their mouths, and hid behind her. She started for the house, leading me by the hand, the children tagging after. When we got there, she set me down on a chair and put herself on a little low stool in front of me, holding both my hands.

"Now I can have a *good* look at you. We been expecting you a couple of days. What kept you?—boat get aground?"

"Yes'm—she—"

"Don't say yes'm—say Aunt Sally. Where did she get aground?"

I didn't know what to say, because I didn't know whether the boat would be coming up the river or down. Then I struck an idea.

"It wasn't the grounding—that didn't keep us back long. We blowed out a cylinder-head."

"Good gracious! Anybody hurt?"

"No'm. Killed a slave."

"Well, that's lucky. Sometimes people do get hurt. Your uncle has been up to town every day to meet you. And he went again, not more than an hour ago. He'll be back any minute now. You must have met him down along the road, didn't you?—oldish man with a—"

"No, I didn't see anybody, Aunt Sally."

"Who did you give your baggage to?"

"Nobody."

"Why, child, it will be stolen!"

"Not where I hid it, it won't."

I was getting so uneasy I could hardly listen. I had my mind on the children, too. I wanted to get them out to one side and pump them a little, to find out who I was. But Mrs. Phelps kept running on. Pretty soon she made the cold chills streak all down my back, when she said:

"But you haven't told me a word about Sis. Now, just tell me *everything*—tell me all about them all."

I was up a stump. I said to myself, "Here's another place where I got to risk the truth." I opened my mouth to begin, but she grabbed me and hustled me behind the bed, and said:

"Here he comes! Stick your head down out of sight. I'll play a joke on him. Children, don't say a word."

The old gentleman walked in and Mrs. Phelps jumped for him and said:

"Has he come?"

"No," said her husband.

"Goodness gracious!" she said, "what in the world can have become of him?"

"I can't imagine," said the old gentleman. "And I must say it makes me dreadful uneasy."

"Uneasy!" she said. "I'm ready to go crazy! He must have come and you missed him along the road. Something *tells* me it is so."

"Why, Sally, I *couldn't* miss him along the road—you know that."

"Oh dear, what *will* Sis say! He must have come! You must have missed him."

"Oh, don't distress me any more than I am already. Something must have happened to the boat. I'm right down scared."

"Why Silas! Look yonder!—up the road!—ain't that somebody coming?"

He rushed to look, and when he turned his back, she stooped down quick and pulled me out. When he turned back from the window, she was smiling like a house afire, holding me by the hand. The old gentleman stared and said:

"Why, who is that?"

"Who do you think it is?"

"I have no idea. Who is it?"

"This is *Tom Sawyer!*"

By jings, I almost slumped through the floor! The old man grabbed me by the hand and shook, and kept on shaking. And then how they both did fire off questions about Tom's brother Sid and his Aunt Polly and the rest of the tribe.

It was like being born again, I was so glad to find out who I was. They froze to me for two hours, and I told them more about my family—I mean the Sawyer family—than ever happened to any six Sawyer families.

By and by I heard a steamboat coughing along down the river. I said to myself, "Suppose Tom Sawyer comes down on that boat? Suppose he steps in here any minute and calls out my name before I can throw him a wink to keep quiet? I must go up the road and waylay him! So I said I would go up to town and get my baggage. The old gentleman was for going along with me, but I said no, I could bring it myself and I'd rather he wouldn't take trouble about me.

Before I was halfway to town I saw somebody coming. Sure enough it was Tom Sawyer. I stopped and waited until he had come up. When he saw me his mouth opened up like a trunk, and stayed so. He swallowed two or three times, and then he said:

"I never harmed you. You know that. What do you want to come back and haunt *me* for?"

I said, "I haven't come back—I haven't been *gone.*"

When he heard my voice it righted him up some, but he wasn't quite sure yet. He said:

"Don't you play tricks on me, because I wouldn't on you. Honest Injun, you are not a ghost?"

"Honest Injun, I'm not."

"Looky here, you haven't been murdered at all?"

"No, I never was murdered at all. You feel of me, if you think I'm a ghost."

Well, wasn't he glad to see me again! I told him the fix I was in, and asked what we had better do. He thought a minute and then said:

"I've got it. You take my baggage and let on it's yours. I'll come a little later. When I come don't you let on to know me."

I said, "All right; but wait a minute. There's one more thing—a thing that nobody knows about but me. And that is, there's a slave here that I'm trying to steal out of slavery. His name is Jim—old Miss Watson's Jim."

He said "What! Why, Jim is—" He stopped and went to studying.

I said: "I know what you'll say. You'll say it's dirty, low-down business. But what if it is? I *am* low down. I'm going to steal him, and I want you to keep mum and not let on. Will you?"

His eyes lit up and he said, "I'll *help* you steal him!"

I couldn't believe it! Tom Sawyer a slave stealer! "Oh, shucks!" I said, "you're joking!"

"I'm not joking, either."

I am bound to say Tom Sawyer fell quite a bit, in my opinion of him.

Well, I went back to the Phelps's place. I got there a heap too quick for that length of the trip, and had to do some explaining. It wasn't hard. The old man was the best, most innocent old soul I ever saw. He wasn't only a farmer; he was a preacher too. He had a little log church on the plantation, that he built himself for a church and a schoolhouse. He never charged anything for his preaching, and it was worth it, too.

25 The Pitiful Ending of Royalty

About half an hour after I got back, Aunt Sally looked out and saw Tom coming up.

"Why, somebody is coming. I wonder who it is? I do believe it's a stranger. Jimmy" (that was one of the children) "run and tell Lize to put on another plate for dinner."

Everybody made a rush for the front door. Strangers didn't come there every day.

Tom could always put on the right style. When he saw us all bunched in the front door, he lifted his hat so dainty, like taking the lid off a box that had butterflies asleep in it. He bowed and said:

"Mr. Archibald Nichols, I believe?"

"No, my boy," said the old gentleman. "I'm sorry. Nichols's place is down a matter of three miles more. Come in, come in. Eat your dinner with us, and then we'll hitch up and take you down to Nichols's."

"Oh, I can't make so much trouble—I couldn't think of it. I'll go on—I don't mind the distance."

"Oh, *do* come in," said Aunt Sally. "You won't be a bit of trouble to us, not a bit in the world. You *must* stay. It's a long dusty three miles to Nichols's. And besides, I have already put on another plate. Come right in and make yourself at home."

Tom thanked them, and let himself be persuaded to come in. When he was in, he said he was a stranger from Hicksville, Ohio. His name was William Thompson—and he made another bow.

He went on and on, making up more stuff about Hicksville and everybody in it. I was getting a little nervous, wondering how this was going to help me out of my scrape. At last, still talking along, he reached over and kissed Aunt Sally right on the mouth. Then he settled back again in his chair, and was going on talking. But she jumped up and wiped her mouth with the back of her hand, and said:

"You owdacious puppy!"

He looked kind of hurt, and said, "I'm surprised at you, ma'am."

"You are surprised—why, what do you reckon *I* am? I've a good notion to take and—Say, what do you mean by kissing me?"

He looked kind of humble, and said, "I didn't mean any harm. I—I—thought you'd like it."

"Why, you born fool!" She took up the spinning-stick and it seemed all she could do to keep from giving him a crack with it. "What made you think I'd like it?"

"Well, I don't know. Only, they—they—told me you would."

"*They* told you I would. Whoever told you is *another* lunatic. Who is *they?*"

"Why, everybody. They all said so, ma'am."

It was all she could do to hold in. Her eyes snapped, and her fingers worked like she wanted to scratch him. "Who is *everybody?* Out with their names, or there'll be one idiot less."

He got up and looked distressed, and fumbled his hat, and said:

"I'm sorry, and I wasn't expecting it. They told me to. They all told me to. But I'm sorry, ma'am, and I won't do it again—I won't, honest."

"You won't, won't you? Well, I should *reckon* you won't!"

"No'm, I'm honest about it. I won't ever do it again—till you ask me."

"Till I *ask* you! Well, I never saw the beat of you in my born days! You'll be as old as Methuselah before *I* ask you—or the likes of you."

"Well," he said, "I'm surprised. I can't make it out. They said you would, and I thought you would. But—" He stopped and looked around for a friendly eye somewhere. He looked at the old gentleman and said, "Didn't *you* think she would like me to kiss her, sir?"

"Why, no; I—I—well, no, I believe I didn't."

Then he looked at me, and said: "Tom, didn't *you* think Aunt Sally would open out her arms and say, 'Sid Sawyer—' "

"My land!" she said, jumping for him, "you impudent young rascal, to fool a body so—"

She was going to hug him, but he fended her off, and said:

"No, not till you have asked me first."

She didn't lose any time, but asked him. She hugged and kissed him again and again, and then turned him over to the old man. After a while Aunt Sally said:

"Why, dear me, I never saw such a surprise. We didn't look for *you* at all, but only Tom. Sis didn't write to me about anybody coming but Tom."

"I begged to come, and at the last minute she let me. Coming down the river, we thought it would be fun for Tom to come in first, and for me to drop in later and let on to be a stranger. But it was a mistake, Aunt Sally. This is no healthy place for a stranger to come to."

"No—not for impudent whelps, Sid. You ought to have your jaws boxed. But I don't care. I would be willing to stand a thousand such jokes to have you here. Well, to think of that performance! I was most petrified with astonishment when you gave me that smack."

We had dinner out in the broad open passage between the house and the kitchen. There was food enough on the table for seven families, and all good and hot. Uncle Silas said a long blessing over it, but it was worth it.

There was a good deal of talk all the afternoon, but not a word about a run-away slave. But at supper that night one of the little boys said:

"Pa, can we go to the show?"

"No. There won't be any show, and you couldn't go anyway. That run-away slave told all about that show, and the people in town know it. I reckon the loafers will be run out of town."

So there it was! Right after supper I said I was tired, and Tom said he was too. We said good-night, went upstairs, climbed out the window and down the lightning rod, and shoved for the town. On the road Tom told me all about how I was murdered, and how Pap dropped out of sight soon after, and what a stir there was when Jim run away. I told Tom about our *Royal Nonesuch* rapscallions, and as much of the raft voyage as I had time to tell.

As we struck into town and up through the middle of it, here comes a rush of people with torches, and awful whooping and yelling, and banging tin pans, and blowing horns. We jumped to one side, and as the crowd went by I saw the king and the duke astraddle a rail, and so all over tar and feathers they didn't look like humans. I was so sorry for the poor rascals I couldn't ever again feel any hardness against them. It was a dreadful thing to see. Human beings *can* be awful cruel to one another.

We poked along back home. I was feeling kind of humble and to blame somehow, though I hadn't done anything. But that is always the way. A person's conscience hasn't got any sense at all. It takes up more room than all the rest of a person's insides, and what is the good of it?

By and by, Tom said, "Looky here, Huck. What fools we have been not to think of it before! I bet I know where Jim is."

"No! Where?"

"In that cabin down by the ash-hopper. Why, looky here, during dinner I saw a slave go in there with a plate of food. What do you think it was for?"

"For a dog."

"Well, it wasn't for a dog. Because part of it was watermelon."

What a head! If I had Tom Sawyer's head I wouldn't trade it off to be a duke, or even a clown in a circus.

"He unlocked the door to go in. Watermelon shows man, lock shows prisoner. All right—I'm glad we found it out detective fashion. I wouldn't give shucks for any other way. Now you work your mind and study out a plan to steal Jim. I'll study out one, too. We'll take the one we like the best. Now start thinking." Pretty soon he said, "Ready?"

"Yes," I said.

"All right—bring out your plan."

"My plan is this," I said. "First, find out if it's Jim in there. If it is, then get up my canoe tomorrow night and go bring my raft over from the island. Then the first dark night that comes, steal the key and get Jim out. Then shove off down the river on the raft, hiding daytimes and running nights, the way we used to do. Wouldn't that plan work?"

"Certainly it would work, like rats a-fighting. But it's too blame simple—there's nothing *to* it. It's mild as goose milk. Easy as breaking into a soap factory."

I didn't say anything. I was expecting the right plan to come from him. And it wouldn't be too simple, either.

When he told me his plan I saw in a minute it was worth fifteen of mine for style. It would make Jim just as free as mine would, and maybe get us all killed besides. I needn't tell what it was yet, for he would be changing it all along, putting new style into it whenever he got a chance.

When we got home the house was all dark. We went on down to the cabin by the ash-hopper to look it over. The hounds didn't make much noise; they had seen us enough to know us. On one side of the cabin we found a window hole, with just one board nailed across it. I said:

"This hole is big enough for Jim to get through if we tear off the board."

Tom said, "I should *hope* we can find a better way than *that,* Huck. That would be easy as playing hooky."

"Well, then," I said, "how will it do to saw him out, the way I got out before I was murdered that time?"

"That would be good, but I bet we can find a better way. No hurry; let's keep on looking around."

On the back side was a lean-to that joined the hut at the eaves. We went in the lean-to and struck a match. There was no door from the lean-to into the cabin. The floor was the ground, and there was nothing in there but some old rusty hoes and spades and picks. Tom was joyful.

"Now we are all right! We can *dig* him out. It'll take about a week!"

Then we started for the house. I went in the back door; you only had to pull a latch-string; they didn't fasten the doors. But that was too easy for Tom Sawyer. No way would do him but he must climb up the lightning-rod. He got up halfway three times, and fell every time. The last time he nearly busted his brains out, and he thought he might have to give it up. But after he was rested he said he'd give her one more try for luck, and this time he made the trip.

26 *Deep-laid Plans*

In the morning we got up at daybreak, and went down to the cabins to pet the dogs and make friends with the man that fed Jim—if it *was* Jim that was being fed. The slaves had just got through breakfast and begun starting for the fields. One named Nat was piling up a tin pan with food. He had a good-natured, chuckle-headed face, and his hair was all tied up in little bunches with thread. That was to keep witches off. He said witches had been pestering him nights, making him see strange things and hear strange noises, and he didn't believe he was ever witched so long before in his life.

"Taking that to feed the dogs?" Tom asked.

A smile spread gradually over Nat's face. "Yes, Mars Sid, a curious dog. Does you want to go and look at him?"

"Yes."

I nudged Tom and whispered, "You going, right here in daylight?"

But he just went along. When we got in the cabin, we could hardly see anything, it was so dark. But Jim was there, sure enough, and he sung out:

"Why, Huck! And good land! ain't that Mars Tom?"

Nat busted in and said, "Why, gracious sakes! do dis here runaway know you gentlemen?"

I had expected it. I didn't know what to do. But Tom looked at him kind of wondering and said:

"I don't reckon he does. What put that into your head?"

"Didn't he dis minute say he knowed you?"

Tom said in a puzzled-up kind of way, "When did he say anything?" He turned to me. "Did *you* hear anybody say anything?"

"No, I didn't hear anybody say anything."

Tom turned to Jim and said, "Did you say anything?"

"No, sah," said Jim. "I ain't said a word."

"Did you ever see us before?"

"No, sah; not as I knows on."

Nat looked wild and distressed. "Oh, de dadblame witches is after me again. I wisht I was dead!"

Tom handed him a dime and told him to buy some more thread to tie up his hair with. While Nat stepped to the door to look at the dime and bite it to see if it was good, Tom whispered to Jim:

"Don't let on to know us. And if you hear digging going on, it will be us. We are going to set you free."

It would be an hour yet till breakfast, so we left and struck down into the woods. Tom said:

"Blame it, this whole thing is too easy. No dog to give sleeping-mixture to. No watchman to be drugged. And Uncle Silas trusts the key to that punkin head. Jim could have got out of that window by this time. Why, drat it, Huck, we got to invent *all* the trouble. Well, first we got to have tools."

"Tools for what?"

"Why, to dig with. We are not going to gnaw him out, are we?"

"The old crippled picks and shovels in the leanto ought to be good enough to dig a slave out with."

He turned on me, looking pitying enough to make a body cry. "Huck Finn, did you *ever* hear of a prisoner having picks and shovels to dig himself out with? Why, you might as well get him the key and be done with it. What we want is a couple of case-knives."

"To dig under that cabin with? Confound it, Tom, that would be foolish!"

"That's the regular way. There's no other way that I ever heard of, and I've read all the books that tell about these things. They always dig out with a case-knife. And not through dirt, mind you, but generally through solid rock. And it takes them weeks and weeks. Why, look at that prisoner in the Castle of Deef, that dug himself out that way. How long was *he* at it?"

"I don't know."

"Well, guess."

"A month and a half?"

"*Thirty-seven years.* And he came out in China."

"Jim wouldn't know anybody in China."

"What has *that* got to do with it?"

"All right. I don't care where he comes out, so as he comes out. Jim won't either, I reckon. But Jim is too old to be dug out with a case-knife. He won't last."

"Yes he will last, too. It won't take thirty-seven years to dig through a *dirt* foundation."

"How long will it take, Tom?"

"Well, we can't be as long as we ought to. Uncle Silas will hear from down there by New Orleans that Jim isn't from there. Then his next move will be to advertise Jim."

"Well, I'll mosey in and snatch a couple of case-knives."

"Snatch three of 'em. We need one to make a saw out of."

"Tom," I said, "there is an old rusty saw blade sticking under the weather-boarding behind the smokehouse."

He looked kind of weary, and said: "Run along now and snatch the knives, three of them."

That night we went down the lightning-rod and shut ourselves up in the lean-to and went to work. We cleared everything out of the way along the middle of the bottom log of the cabin. Tom said that place was right behind Jim's bed, and we'd dig in under it. When we got through, the hole wouldn't be seen in the cabin, because Jim's bed cover hung down to the ground.

We dug and dug with the case-knives till almost midnight. Our hands got blisters. And yet you couldn't see we had done anything hardly. At last I said:

"This is no thirty-seven year job. This is a thirty-eight year job, Tom Sawyer."

Tom sighed, and pretty soon he stopped digging. "We got to dig him out with picks, and *let on* we do it with case-knives. Give me a case-knife."

He had his own by him, but I handed him mine. He flung it down and said:

"Give me a *case-knife.*"

At first I didn't know just what to do. Then I thought. I handed him a pickax. He took it and went to work without saying a word. Then I got a shovel, and we picked and shoveled, turn about, for about half an hour, which was as long as we could stand up. But we had a good deal of a hole to show for it.

I went in through the back door. When I got upstairs, I looked out the window and saw Tom doing his level best to climb up the lightning-rod. But he couldn't make it, his hands were so sore. I said:

"Come in at the back door and let on that the stairway is a lightning-rod."

So he did.

The next night we went down the lightning-rod a little after ten, and took one of the candles along. We listened under the window of the cabin and heard Jim snoring. Then we whirled in with the pick and shovel, and in about two hours the job was done. We crept in and pawed around and found a candle and lit it. Then we woke Jim up. He was so glad to see us he almost cried. He called us honey, and all the pet names he could think of.

Tom told Jim not to be the least afraid, because we would see he got away, sure. Then Tom thought of something.

"You got any spiders in here, Jim?"

"No, sah, thanks to goodness, Mars Tom."

"All right, we'll get you some."

"But bless you, honey, I don't want none. I's afeard of 'em."

"You got any rats around here?"

"No, sah, I ain't seen none."

"Well, we'll get you some rats."

"Why, Mars Tom, I don't want no rats. No, sah, gimme garter snakes if I's got to have somethin', but don't gimme no rats."

"But, Jim, you *got* to have rats—all prisoners do. And they train and pet them, and play music to them. You got anything to play music on?"

"Nothin' but a juice-harp."

"Plenty good enough for rats. You can play to them before you go to sleep and early in the morning. And when you do, you'll see—all the rats and the snakes and the spiders will just fairly swarm out."

Jim found so much fault with jew's-harping the rats, and petting up the snakes and spiders, that Tom almost lost patience with him. Jim said it was more worry to be prisoner than to be free.

In the morning we got a wire rat-trap and unstopped the best rat-hole. In about an hour we had fifteen bully ones. Then we took the trap full of rats and put it in a safe place under Aunt Sally's bed, while we went for spiders. Before we got back one of the children found it there and opened the door of it to see if the rats would come out, and they did. When we got back Aunt Sally was standing on top of the bed raising Cain. She dusted us both with the hickory.

We got a splendid stock of spiders and bugs and frogs and caterpillars. We almost got a hornets' nest, but we didn't. The family was at home.

We got some garter snakes and put them in a bag and took it to our room. When we went back upstairs after supper, there wasn't a blessed snake there. They had worked out of the bag somehow, and left. There was no real scarcity of snakes about the house for quite a spell. You would see them dripping from the rafters, and every now and then one landed in your plate, or down the back of your neck. Everyone of them was handsome and striped, and there wasn't any harm in a million of them. But that made no difference to Aunt Sally. Every time one of them flopped down on her, no difference what she was doing, she would just lay her work down and light out. And you could hear her whoop to Jericho. If she turned over and found one in bed, she let out such a howl you would think the house was afire. I never saw such a woman. Why, it was a week before she was over it. You could touch her on the back of her neck with a feather, and she would jump right out of her stockings.

We got a licking every time one of our snakes got in her way. I didn't mind the lickings, because they didn't amount to anything, but I minded the trouble we had to lay in another supply of snakes. But we laid them in, and you never saw a cabin as lively as Jim's was. He said that between the spiders and the rats and the snakes, there wasn't room for him. He said if he ever got out this time he wouldn't be a prisoner again for a salary.

27 A Mixed-up and Splendid Rescue

Uncle Silas wrote a couple of times to the plantation below Orleans, telling the owner to come and get the runaway slave. He never had an answer, because there was no such plantation.

Then he said he would advertise Jim in the St. Louis and New Orleans papers. When he said the St. Louis papers, I got the cold shivers. I saw we didn't have any time to lose. Tom said it was time for the 'nonymous letters.*

"What's that?" I said.

"Warnings to the people that something is up."

"But looky here, Tom, what do we want to warn anybody for? Let them find it out themselves—it'll be their lookout."

"Why, they're so mullet-headed, they don't take notice of anything. If we don't *give* them warning there won't be anybody or anything to interfere with us. The escape will go off flat—nothing to it."

"Well, as for me, Tom, I think that's the way I'd like it."

"Shucks!" he said, and looked weary with me.

So Tom wrote the 'nonymous letter, and shoved it under the front door. It said:

* "Anonymous" letters do not have the writer's name signed.

Beware!
Trouble is brewing!
Keep a sharp lookout!

Unknown
Friend.

Then we took some blood and made a picture of a skull and crossbones, and tacked it on the front door.

The next night we put a picture of a coffin on the back door.

I never saw a family in such a sweat. They couldn't have been worse scared if the place had been full of ghosts. If a door banged, Aunt Sally jumped and said "Ouch!" If anything fell, she jumped. If you happened to touch her when she wasn't looking, she jumped.

Next night we got another letter ready. We didn't know where to put it, because we had heard them say at supper that a servant would be on watch at both doors all night. Tom went down the lightning-rod to spy around. The servant at the back door was asleep. So he stuck the letter down the back of his neck. The letter said:

A gang of cuthroats from over in
the Indian territory is going to steal
your runway slave tonight and they
have been trying to scare you so you
will stay in the house and not bother
them. I am one of the gang but I have
got religgion and am going to quit
it and lead an honest life again.
they will sneak along the fence at
midnight exact with a false key
and go in the cabin to get him. I am to
be off a piece and blow a tin horn
if I see any danger. But stead
of that I will ba like a sheep
soon as they get in the cabin. while
they are getting his chains loose you
slip there and lock them in and kill
them at your leasure. Don't do anything
but just the way I tell you or they will
suspect and raise whoop-jamboreehoo.
I don't want any reward but to
know I have done right.

Unknown Friend.

Next morning after breakfast, we took my canoe and went over the river fishing. We carried along a lunch, and had a good time. We took a look at the raft and found her all right. We got home late to supper. Everybody was in such a sweat and worry they didn't know which end they stood on. They made us go right off to bed the minute we had done supper and wouldn't tell us what the trouble was. They didn't say a word about the last letter, but didn't need to.

Halfway upstairs we turned and slid to the cellar cupboard, and loaded up a good lunch. We took it up to our room and went to bed. About half-past eleven we got up and got ready to start. Tom said:

"Where is the butter? You must have left it downstairs!"

"We can get along without it," I said.

"We can get along *with* it, too. Just you slide down cellar and get it. I'll go on down the lightning-rod and wait for you outside."

So out he went, and down cellar I went. The hunk of butter, big as a person's fist, was where I had left it. I took it up, put out my light, and started upstairs very quiet. I got to the main floor all right. Then here comes Aunt Sally with a candle. I clapped the butter in my hat and clapped my hat on my head. The next second she saw me.

"What you been *doing* down cellar?"

"Nothing."

"Well, then, what made you go down there this time of night?"

"I don't know, ma'am."

"Don't answer me that way, Tom. I want to know what you been *doing* down there. You just march into that front room and stay there till I come. You been up to something you had no business to. I intend to find out what it is before I'm done with you."

She went away, and I opened the door and walked into the front room. My, but there was a crowd there! Fifteen farmers, and every one of them had a gun. I was so sick I slunk to a chair.

The men talked a little in low voices, and all seemed uneasy but trying to hide it. They kept taking off their hats, and putting them on, and scratching their heads, and changing their seats, and fumbling with their buttons. I wasn't easy myself, but I didn't take my hat off, all the same. I did wish Aunt Sally would come and lick me if she wanted to, so I could get away and tell Tom how we had overdone this thing. We had got ourselves into a thundering hornets' nest. We had better stop fooling around now, and clear out with Jim before these men got out of patience and went for us.

At last Aunt Sally walked into the room and began to ask me questions. I was shaking all over and ready to sink in my tracks, I was so scared. The men had gone into such a fidget by now that some of them wanted to start, saying it was only a few minutes to midnight. And here was Aunt Sally pegging away at the questions. The place got hotter and hotter, and the butter commenced to melt and run down my neck and behind my ears. One of the men said:

"I'm for going to the cabin right *now.*"

I almost dropped. A streak of butter trickled down my forehead. Aunt Sally saw it, snatched off my hat, and out comes the butter. She grabbed and hugged me, and said:

"Dear, dear, why didn't you *tell* me what you had been down there for! I wouldn't have cared. Now clear out to bed. Don't let me see you till morning!"

In a second I was upstairs, down the lightning-rod, and shinning through the dark for the lean-to. I could hardly get the words out, I was so breathless, but I told Tom as quick as I could that we hadn't a minute to lose—the house was full of men with guns!

His eyes just blazed. "Bully! Why, Huck, if it was to do over again, I bet I could bring in two hundred men!"

"Hurry! hurry!" I said. "Where is Jim?"

"Right at your elbow. Now we'll slide out."

Just then we heard the tromp of men coming. They walked right up to the cabin and fumbled with the padlock. One man said:

"They haven't come yet—the door is still locked."

Tom put his eye to a crack of the lean-to door, but couldn't make out anything, it was so dark. He set his ear to the crack and listened and listened. At last he nudged us and we slid out, stooping down, not breathing or making the least noise, going toward the fence in single file. I got over all right and so did Jim, but Tom's britches caught fast on a splinter of the top rail. He heard steps coming and had to pull loose in such a hurry, the splinter snapped and made a noise. Somebody sung out:

"Who's that? Answer, or I'll shoot!"

We didn't answer. We just unfurled our heels and shoved. Then there was a rush and a *bang, bang, bang!* The bullets fairly whizzed around us. We heard them sing out:

"There they go!" "They've started for the river!" "After them, boys, and turn loose the dogs!"

So here they come, full tilt. We could hear them, because they wore boots and yelled. But we didn't wear boots and didn't yell. We dodged into the bush and let them go by, then dropped in behind them.

They'd had all the dogs shut up, so they wouldn't scare off the robbers. But by this time somebody had let them loose, and they went running around making powwow enough for a million. We stopped in our tracks till the dogs caught up. When they saw it was nobody but us—with no excitement to offer them—they just said howdy and tore right ahead, toward the shouting and clattering.

We whizzed along after them till nearly to the mill. Then we struck up through the bush to where my canoe was tied, hopped in and pulled for dear life toward the island where the raft was.

At first we could hear yelling and barking all up and down the river bank, but as we moved on, the sounds got dim and died out. Then I said:

"Now, old Jim, you are a free man again!"

Everybody was glad as could be, but Tom was the gladdest of all, because he had a bullet in the calf of his leg. His leg was hurting some and bleeding. We put him in the wigwam and tore up one of the duke's shirts to bandage him. Then we told him I was going for a doctor. He raised a row against it, but we stuck to it.

28 *Why They Didn't Hang Jim*

The doctor was an old man, a very nice, kind-looking old man, when I got him up. I told him we had been hunting over on Spanish Island yesterday afternoon, and had camped on a piece of a raft we found. About midnight my brother must have kicked his gun in his dreams, for it went off and shot him in the leg. Would he fix it and not let anybody know about it, for we wanted to come home and surprise the folks?

"Who are your folks?" he said.

"The Phelpses, down yonder."

"Oh," he said. And after a minute, "How did you say he got shot?"

"He had a dream," I said, "and it shot him."

"Strange dream," he said.

So he lit up his lantern and got his bag, and we started. But when he saw the canoe, he said she didn't look safe for two. I said:

"Oh, you needn't be afraid, sir. She carried the three of us easy enough."

"What three?"

"Why me, and Sid, and—and—and the guns."

"Oh," he said.

But he put his foot on the boat and rocked her, and shook his head. So he took my canoe, and said for me to wait till he got back. Or maybe I had better go home and get them ready for the surprise. I told him how to find the raft, and then he started.

I crept into a lumber pile to get some sleep. Next time I waked up, the sun was away up over my head! I shot out and went for the doctor's house. They told me he had gone away in the night some time or other, and hadn't come back yet. Well, I thought, that looks bad for Tom, and I'll get out to the island right off.

I turned the corner and nearly rammed my head into Uncle Silas's stomach! He said:

"Why, Tom! Where you been all this time, you rascal?"

"I haven't been anywhere. Only hunting for the runaway slave—with Sid."

"Where ever did you go?" he said. "Your Aunt has been mighty uneasy."

"She needn't," I said. "We followed the men and the dogs, but they outran us, and we lost them. We thought we heard them on the water, so we got a canoe and took out after them and crossed over. Then we cruised along up shore till we got kind of tired and beat out. So we tied up the canoe and went to sleep and didn't wake up till about an hour ago. We paddled over to hear the news. Sid is at the post-office."

Uncle Silas said we'd go to the post-office and get him. But just as I expected, he wasn't there. The old man got a letter out of the office, and said:

"Come along, let Sid foot it home, or canoe it, when he gets done fooling around."

I couldn't get him to let me stay and wait for Sid. When we got home Aunt Sally was so glad to see me she laughed and cried both, and let me have one of her lickings that didn't amount to shucks. She said she'd serve Sid the same when he got home.

The place was plumb full of farmers and farmers' wives, and such another clack was never heard, tongues going all the time. When it was late in the day, the people all left. Pretty soon Aunt Sally jumped up, and said:

"Why, laws a-mercy, it's 'most night, and Sid not come yet! What *has* become of that boy?"

"I'll run right up to town and get him," I said.

"No you won't. You stay right where you are. *One* is enough to be lost at a time. If he's not here by supper, your Uncle will go."

Well, he wasn't there to supper, so right after supper Uncle went. It was ten o'clock before he was back, a little bit uneasy, for he hadn't run across track of Tom. Aunt Sally was a good deal uneasy. Uncle Silas said no need to worry—boys will be boys, and he'll turn up in the morning all sound and right.

She said she'd stay up for him a while anyway, and keep a light burning so he could see it. When I went to bed, she went along with me, and tucked me in so good I felt mean and couldn't look her in the face. When she was leaving, she looked down in my eyes so gentle, and said:

"The door won't be locked, Tom, and there is the window and the lightning-rod. But you'll be good, won't you? You won't go? For *my* sake?"

Laws knows I *wanted* to go bad enough, to see about Tom, and had intended to go. But after that I wouldn't have gone, not for kingdoms.

But she was on my mind, and Tom was on my mind, so I slept very restless. Twice I went down the lightning-rod and slipped around front, to see her there by the candle in the window. I wished I could do something for her, but all I could do was to swear I'd never again do anything to grieve her. The third time I waked up it was dawn. I slipped down, and she was there yet, her old gray head resting on her hand. She was asleep.

The old man was up town again before breakfast, but couldn't get track of Tom. After breakfast both of them stayed at the table thinking, not eating anything, but looking mournful, their coffee getting cold. By and by the old man said:

"Did I give you that letter?"

"What letter?"

"The one I got yesterday out of the post-office."

"No, you didn't give me any letter."

"I must have forgot it."

He felt his pockets, brought out the letter and handed it to her.

"Why, it's from St. Petersburg—it's from Sis."

I thought a walk would do me good, but I couldn't stir. But before she could break the letter open, she dropped it and went tearing out, for she'd seen something.

It was Tom Sawyer on a mattress, and that old doctor, and Jim with his hands tied behind him, and a lot of other people. I hid the letter behind the first thing that was handy, and rushed out. Aunt Sally flung herself at Tom, crying, and said:

"Oh, he's dead, he's dead, I know he is!"

Tom turned his head a little, and muttered something that showed he wasn't in his right mind. Then she flung up her hands, and said:

"He's alive, thank God!" And away she went to get the bed ready, throwing orders right and left, as fast as her tongue could go. The old doctor and Uncle Silas followed after Tom into the house.

I followed the men who had Jim, to see what they meant to do with him. Some of them wanted to hang him, as an example not to run away. But the others said, "No, he ain't ours—his owner will turn up and make us pay for him, sure." That idea cooled them down a little. But they fetched him a cuff or two on the head, and cussed him.

Jim never said a word. He didn't let on to know me. They took him to the same cabin, and said he wasn't to have anything to eat but bread and water till his owner claimed him, or he was sold at auction if he never was claimed. About this time the old doctor comes to take a look, and said:

"Don't be rougher on him than you have to be. He's not bad. When I found the wounded boy, I saw I couldn't cut the bullet out without some help, and he was in no state to be left alone while I went for help. He was out of his head, wouldn't let me come near him. Then out crawls this runaway slave from somewhere and says he'll help. And he did too. I had to stick there till daylight this morning, and I never saw a better nurse. And he was risking his freedom to do it. I liked him for that! I tell you, gentlemen, a slave like that is worth kind treatment."

The men softened up a little. I judged I would get the doctor's story to Aunt Sally, so Jim wouldn't have to live on bread and water. But first I would have to get through the breakers just ahead of me. How was I to explain why I forgot to mention about Sid being shot, when I was telling how we put in that dratted night paddling around hunting for a runaway?

But I had plenty of time. Aunt Sally stuck to the sickroom all day and all night. And every time I saw Uncle Silas mooning around, I dodged him.

29 *Nothing More to Write*

Next morning I heard that Tom was a good deal better. They said Aunt Sally had gone to get a nap, so I slipped to the sickroom. If I found Tom awake, we might put up a story for the family that would wash. But he was sleeping, and sleeping quiet; and he was pale, not fire-faced the way he was when they brought him home. I thought I'd wait for him to wake.

After a while Aunt Sally glided in, and there I was, up a stump! She motioned me to be still, and we both stayed there, watching Tom. By and by he stirred, and opened his eyes very natural, and said:

"Hello! Why, I'm at home! How is that? Where is the raft?"

"It's all right," I said.

"And Jim?"

"The same," I said, but couldn't say it very brash.

"Good! Did you tell Aunt Sally?"

I was going to say yes, but she chipped in.

"About what?"

"About how we set the slave free."

"Good land! What is the child talking about! Dear, dear, out of his head again!"

"No, I'm not out of my head—I know all I'm talking about. We *did* set him free. We planned it all by ourselves. We dug the hole into the cabin, and wrote the 'nonymous letters from the robbers." He'd got a good start, and she didn't check him, just stood there and stared and let him clip along. I saw it wasn't any use for *me* to put in.

"Well, I never heard the like of it in all my born days! So it was you, you little rapscallions, that made all this trouble and scared us all to death. I've a good notion to take it out of you this very minute. You just get well once, you young scamp, and I'll tan the Old Harry out of both of you!"

Tom was so proud he couldn't hold in, and his tongue just *went* it—she chipping in, and spitting fire all along.

"Well, you get all the fun you can out of it *now*. But mind, if I catch you meddling with that runaway again—"

Tom looked at me and said, "Didn't you just say that Jim was all right? Didn't he get away?"

" 'Deed he didn't," said Aunt Sally. "He's in that cabin again, on bread and water. And he'll be there until he's claimed or sold!"

Tom rose square up in bed, his eyes hot. "They have no *right* to shut him up. Turn him loose! He's as free as any creature that walks the earth!"

"What *does* the child mean?"

"I mean every word I say. Old Miss Watson died before I left St. Petersburg. She said she was ashamed she had ever thought of selling him down the river and she set him free in her will."

"Then what on earth did you want to set him free for, if he was already free!"

"Why—I wanted the *adventure* of it. I'd have waded neck deep in blood to—goodness alive, *Aunt Polly!*"

There was Aunt Polly standing in the door, looking as sweet as an angel half full of pie!

Aunt Sally jumped for her and hugged her and cried over her. I found a good enough place for me under the bed. In a little while I peeped out and saw Aunt Polly looking at Tom—kind of grinding him into the earth.

"Yes, you *better* turn your head away, you Tom."

"Oh, deary me!" said Aunt Sally. "Is he changed so much? That isn't Tom, that's Sid. Tom was here a minute ago. Where did he go?"

"You mean where did Huck Finn go. I haven't raised such a scamp as my Tom all these years not to know him when I see him. Come out from under that bed, Huck Finn."

I crawled out, but not feeling brash.

Tom's Aunt Polly told all about who I was. She said Tom was right about old Miss Watson setting Jim free in her will. Now I could understand how a boy with Tom's bringing up would sink to stealing a slave to set him free.

Aunt Polly said that when Aunt Sally wrote her that Tom *and Sid too* had come all right and safe, she said to herself: "Look at that, now! I might have expected it, letting him go off without anybody to watch him. Now I got to go all the way down the river to find out what that creature is up to *this* time. (Tom, you *do* need skinning, and no mistake about it.) I wrote a letter just before I started to tell you I was coming—"

"Oh, I got that yesterday. I haven't read it yet."

I wanted to offer to bet two dollars she couldn't find it. But I thought it was safer to say nothing.

Aunt Sally was the most mixed-up person I ever saw. Except Uncle Silas. When they told it all to him,

it kind of made him drunk. He didn't know anything at all the rest of the day.

The first time I caught Tom alone I asked him what was the idea of stealing a slave to set him free when he was already free. He said his idea was to run down the river on the raft, and have adventure plumb to the mouth of the river. Then he would tell Jim he was free and take him back on a steamboat in great style.

Well, we had Jim up in Tom's sickroom, and Tom gave him forty dollars for being a prisoner for us. Jim was pleased to death, and said:

"Dah, now, Huck. I *told* you I was bound to be rich one day, and it's come true. Signs is *signs,* I tell you!"

Then Tom said, "Let's all three slide out of here one of these nights, and get an outfit, and go for howling adventures in the Indian Territory, for a couple of weeks."

I said I didn't have any money to buy an outfit, that most likely Pap had come back by now and got all the money away from Judge Thatcher and drunk it up.

Jim said, kind of solemn, "He ain't comin' back no mo', Huck."

"Why, Jim?" I said.

"Never mind why, Huck—but he ain't comin' back no mo'."

I kept at him to tell me why, and at last he said:

"You 'member de house floatin' down de river, and de dead man dat I didn't let you see? Well, dat was him."

Tom is about well now, and wears his bullet on a watch-guard for a watch, and is always seeing what time it is. So there's not anything more to write about, and I'm rotten glad of it. If I had thought what a trouble it is to write a book, I never would have tackled it. And I won't tackle it again.

But I reckon I got to light out for Indian Territory ahead of the others, because Aunt Sally says she's going to adopt me and civilize me. I can't stand that. I been there before.

REVIEWING
YOUR
READING

CHAPTER 1

Finding the Main Idea

1. In this chapter, the author is mainly interested in telling about
   a. what Huck's life is like at the Widow Douglas's   **b.** how Moses was found in the bulrushes   **c.** how Huck and Tom invested their treasure   **d.** Huck's interest in history

Remembering Detail

2. At night, Miss Watson gives Huck lessons in
   a. arithmetic   **b.** piano   **c.** spelling   **d.** astronomy

3. The animal sound Tom and Huck use as a signal is that of
   a. an owl   **b.** a cat   **c.** a possum   **d.** a dog

Drawing Conclusions

4. When Huck says the widow "grumbles a little over her plate" before meals, he means she really is
   a. complaining about the food   **b.** saying a prayer   **c.** trying to remember something   **d.** making conversation

Identifying the Tone

5. Which of the following words best describes Huck's attitude toward life at the Widow Douglas's
   a. carefree   **b.** grateful   **c.** discontented   **d.** contented

THINKING IT OVER

Judging from Huck's reactions to life in Widow Douglas's household, what do you suppose his life was like before he came there to live?

CHAPTER 2

Finding the Main Idea

1. This chapter is mostly about how
   a. Huck escapes from the Widow Douglas's b. Tom, Huck, and their friends organize a secret gang c. the gang members get even with their enemies d. the gang chooses a leader

Remembering Detail

2. To join the gang, each member must
   a. memorize the oath b. commit a serious crime c. make his thumbprint on the oath in blood d. sign his name to the oath in blood

3. The gang can not make its first holdup on Sunday because
   a. Ben Rogers is not free that day b. the boys say it would be wicked to rob and kill on Sunday c. stage coaches operate only on weekdays d. the gang's supplies have not arrived

Appreciating Language

4. The boys are confused about the meaning of *ransom*. To hold a person for ransom means to
   a. mistreat the person b. demand money for the person's release c. force the person to join a gang d. starve the person slowly

Using Logic to Find Deeper Meaning

5. Huck, not having a family, offers to have Miss Watson "killed" probably because
   a. she is the one most like a mother to him b. he is ashamed of his own father c. he would rather sacrifice her than the Widow Douglas, whom he likes better d. she is the first person he thinks of

THINKING IT OVER

The author gives the reader a number of clues to show that the bloodthirsty talk of what the gang will do is pure make-believe. One clue is how Tom and the others react when Tommy Barnes threatens to tell all their secrets. Explain how their actions then contrast with the punishment set forth in the oath they have just agreed to.

CHAPTER 3

Remembering Detail

1. The signal for the gang to get together is
   a. a boy carrying a blazing stick   **b.** the hoot of an owl
   c. a bugle call   **d.** a pistol shot

2. The "band of Spanish merchants and rich A-rabs" turns out to be
   a. a group of magicians   **b.** a traveling circus   **c.** small children on a Sunday School picnic   **d.** a band of gypsies

3. When Huck tries rubbing a tin lamp
   a. a genie appears   **b.** Tom Sawyer appears   **c.** Miss Watson calls him a fool   **d.** nothing happens

Drawing Conclusions

4. You can tell from this chapter that Tom Sawyer
   a. dislikes Sunday School children   **b.** has an active imagination   **c.** can not be tricked by magicians   **d.** is far wiser than Huck

Identifying the Tone

5. Which of the following best describes Huck's feelings as Tom tells him about genies?
   a. excited   **b.** impressed   **c.** skeptical   **d.** bored

THINKING IT OVER

Compare Tom and Huck. Which is the more down-to-earth character? Be able to back up your opinion with examples from the chapter.

CHAPTER 4

Finding the Main Idea
1. The purpose of this chapter is to
   a. explain why Pap stops drinking   **b.** show what Pap is like   **c.** tell about Huck's family background   **d.** show that Pap has been misunderstood

Remembering Detail
2. Huck is warned of Pap's return by
   a. Tom Sawyer   **b.** tracks in the snow that he recognizes   **c.** a message from Judge Thatcher   **d.** a dream

3. Pap takes a dollar from Huck to buy himself
   a. a pair of second-hand shoes   **b.** a new hat   **c.** a good dinner   **d.** whiskey

4. Huck's father goes to court to
   a. get control of Huck's six thousand dollars   **b.** prevent Huck from going to school   **c.** punish the Widow Douglas   **d.** get even with Judge Thatcher

Drawing Conclusions
5. Huck says that he "could say the multiplication table up to six times seven is thirty-five." This suggests that Huck
   a. is a whiz at arithmetic   **b.** needs more work in multiplication   **c.** likes arithmetic better than spelling   **d.** has a poor teacher

Appreciating Language
6. When Huck says Pap *tanned* him so much, he means that Pap
   a. made him work in the sun   **b.** beat him a lot   **c.** swore at him often   **d.** made him work hard

Using Logic to Find Deeper Meaning
7. Pap signs the pledge to stop drinking by making his mark, not by writing his signature, because
   a. that is the custom   **b.** he can't write his name   **c.** his arm is broken   **d.** he doesn't really intend to reform

THINKING IT OVER
Why is Pap so much against Huck's going to school? How does this attitude differ from the attitude of most other parents?

CHAPTER 5

Finding the Main Idea

1. This chapter is mostly about how Huck
   a. misses school   **b.** builds a raft   **c.** gets away from
   Pap   **d.** gets money to give Pap

Remembering Detail

2. When Pap goes to the ferry landing for supplies he always
   a. takes Huck along   **b.** leaves Huck to hunt and fish
   c. ties Huck to the cabin door   **d.** locks Huck in the cabin

3. The tool that enables Huck to escape is a
   a. hammer   **b.** saw   **c.** chisel   **d.** shovel

4. An old blanket was nailed to the cabin wall to
   a. keep anyone from seeing in   **b.** keep the wind from blowing
   out the candle   **c.** shade the sunlight   **d.** provide some color

Identifying the Tone

5. Which of the following best describes Pap's attitude in the passage
   about voting?
   a. friendly   **b.** racist   **c.** curious   **d.** admiring

Using Logic to Find Deeper Meaning

6. Pap's calling himself a man "worth six thousand dollars" shows
   that he
   a. has a savings account   **b.** expects the court to give him control
   of Huck's money   **c.** expects to sell a lot of fish and game
   d. plans to stop drinking and become respectable

THINKING IT OVER

1. Why does Huck decide to live alone on Jackson's Island instead
   of going back to live with the Widow Douglas?

2. Why does Huck go to so much trouble to make people think
   he is dead?

CHAPTER 6

Finding the Main Idea

1. The chapter is mostly about
   a. Pap's search for Huck **b.** Huck's meeting Jim on the island **c.** building a raft **d.** the manhunt for Jim

Remembering Detail

2. The purpose of firing the cannon from the ferry is to
   a. make a dead body rise to the water's surface **b.** warn that a slave has run away **c.** warn other boats that the ferry is coming **d.** stun the catfish

3. Huck stumbles onto the ashes of a campfire as he is
   a. picking berries **b.** gathering firewood **c.** following a snake through the grass **d.** looking for spring water

4. At their first meal together, Huck and Jim eat
   a. strawberries **b.** snake meat **c.** food that Huck has brought from the cabin **d.** game that Huck shoots

5. Most of the signs that Jim knows about foretell
   a. good luck **b.** bad luck **c.** death **d.** weather changes

Drawing Conclusions

6. Jim is terrified at seeing Huck because he
   a. fears Huck will report him **b.** thinks he is seeing a ghost **c.** believes Huck will shoot him **d.** supposes Pap must be nearby

Appreciating Language

7. When Jim says he *lit out,* he means that he
   a. got angry **b.** fainted **c.** left suddenly **d.** started a fire

Using Logic to Find Deeper Meaning

8. The fact that Miss Watson planned to sell Jim shows that
   a. she was willing to break the law for $800 **b.** slavery was legal in Missouri at the time of the story **c.** the story takes place after the Civil War **d.** she wanted to punish him for running away

THINKING IT OVER

Explain how Jim made his escape. Tell why he did not run away on foot or take a boat.

CHAPTER 7

Remembering Detail

1. On Jackson's Island, Huck and Jim find shelter in
   a. an old shack   **b.** a tent   **c.** a cave   **d.** a frame house

2. The river continues to rise for
   a. about twelve hours   **b.** ten or twelve days   **c.** several days
   d. a month

3. The dead man in the frame house had been
   a. drowned   **b.** shot   **c.** stabbed   **d.** hanged

4. When Huck goes ashore for news, he is disguised as a
   a. girl   **b.** widow   **c.** preacher   **d.** gypsy

Drawing Conclusions

5. Huck and Jim travel only at night because
   a. it is cooler then   **b.** the current is less strong at night
   c. they spend the days hunting   **d.** they are afraid of being seen

6. The calico dress Huck uses as a disguise
   a. came from the frame house that floated by   **b.** belonged to
   Miss Watson   **c.** belonged to Becky Thatcher   **d.** was bought
   at the ferry landing

Identifying the Tone

7. Which of the following best describes the life Huck and Jim lead
   on Jackson's Island?
   a. dreary   **b.** happy   **c.** troubled   **d.** unhappy

THINKING IT OVER

Early in this chapter, Huck says "Jim, this is nice. . . . I wouldn't
want to be anywhere else but here." Do you think Huck is sincere?
Would you like to lead the kind of life Huck and Jim have been
leading? Explain.

CHAPTER 8

Finding the Main Idea

1. This chapter is mostly about
   a. how Huck learns the island is no longer safe **b.** how Huck succeeds in fooling Mrs. Loftus **c.** Huck's life on Jackson's Island **d.** the damage caused by the flood

Remembering Detail

2. The reward offered for Jim's capture is
   a. $800 **b.** $50 **c.** $300 **d.** $1,000

3. Mrs. Loftus first guesses that Huck is not a girl because of
   a. his voice **b.** the kind of haircut he has **c.** his shoes
   d. the way he threads a needle

4. Who besides Jim is suspected of being Huck's murderer?
   a. a one-legged man **b.** Pap **c.** Judge Thatcher
   d. Mr. Loftus

Drawing Conclusions

5. Huck does not remove his bonnet in Mrs. Loftus's house because
   a. he doesn't plan to stay long **b.** he's afraid he won't be able to get it back on **c.** he's afraid his haircut will show that he's a boy **d.** he has bad manners

Appreciating Language

6. When Mrs. Loftus calls Huck's father a *hard lot,* she means he is
   a. a bad sort of person **b.** an unlucky person **c.** a lucky person **d.** a hard person to figure out

Using Logic to Find Deeper Meaning

7. When Huck tells Jim, "They are after us!" he uses *us* not *you* because
   a. people have discovered that he hasn't been murdered **b.** he intends to stick with Jim **c.** there is a reward for him as well as for Jim **d.** he can hear bloodhounds on the river bank

THINKING IT OVER

Which of the tests that Mrs. Loftus uses to prove that Huck is a boy, not a girl, do you think would work today? Which one(s) would be less reliable today than at the time of the story? Explain your answers.

CHAPTER 9

Finding the Main Idea

1. This chapter is mostly about
   a. how Huck and Jim leave the island   **b.** what life on the river is like   **c.** how to build a wigwam   **d.** the close call they have as they pass St. Louis

Remembering Detail

2. A *towhead* is
   a. a tree stump in the water   **b.** a sand bar with trees growing on it   **c.** a rock below the surface of the water   **d.** a kind of tree

3. On leaving the island, Huck and Jim load their possessions
   a. all on the raft   **b.** all in the canoe   **c.** into backpacks   **d.** partly on the raft and partly in the canoe

4. Pap says there was no harm in borrowing if
   a. you didn't take too much   **b.** you planned to pay the owner back someday   **c.** you were starving   **d.** you didn't borrow from the same person twice

5. Huck and Jim agree to stop borrowing
   a. watermelons   **b.** sweet corn   **c.** crabapples   **d.** cantaloupes

Appreciating Language

6. When Huck says, "Sometimes I *lifted* a chicken that wasn't roosting comfortable," he means that he
   a. tried to make the chicken more comfortable   **b.** stole the chicken   **c.** took eggs from under the chicken   **d.** set the chicken free

Using Logic to Find Deeper Meaning

7. The big steamboats travel down the Missouri side of the river and up the middle because
   a. the current is stronger near the Missouri shore   **b.** boats are supposed to keep to the left   **c.** boats are supposed to keep to the right   **d.** the current is stronger in the middle

THINKING IT OVER

Huck thinks of what Tom Sawyer would do on seeing the wrecked steamboat. Does he mention Tom in an admiring way? Does he partly make fun of Tom? Explain.

CHAPTER 10

Finding the Main Idea

1. The chapter is mainly about
   a. honor among thieves   **b.** Tom Sawyer's influence on
   Huck   **c.** the adventure on the *Walter Scott*   **d.** rescuing
   passengers from a grounded steamboat

Remembering Detail

2. Jake stops Bill from shooting the third man because he
   a. takes pity on the man   **b.** thinks the man has valuable
   information   **c.** wants to let the man drown so he and Bill will
   not risk a murder charge   **d.** is sure that the man is too frightened
   to tell on them

3. Huck and Jim must take the boat belonging to the men because
   a. their raft has broken loose and floated away   **b.** they don't
   have time to load the loot onto the raft   **c.** their raft is stuck
   on the rocks   **d.** they don't want the men to be able to follow
   them

4. Huck gets the ferryman to go to the wreck because he
   a. hopes to save the lives of the three men   **b.** wants the reward
   for capturing the three men   **c.** promised Miss Hooker he
   would   **d.** is afraid that Jake and Bill will kill the other man
   after all

Identifying the Tone

5. When Jake and Bill enter the room where he is hiding, Huck
   feels
   a. angry   **b.** lonely   **c.** frightened   **d.** seasick

Drawing Conclusions

6. Huck learns the name of the nearby town by
   a. looking at a map   **b.** leading the ferryman to say it   **c.** reading
   it on a signpost   **d.** asking someone

THINKING IT OVER

Do you think it was wrong of Huck and Jim to take the men's
boat, since doing so resulted in the men's death? Explain your answer.

CHAPTER 11

Remembering Detail

1. Jim is sure that if he is sent back to Miss Watson she will
   a. forgive him for running away   **b.** scold him but let him remain in Missouri   **c.** sell him to a plantation in the South   **d.** have him arrested for Huck's murder

2. The conversation about kings begins after Huck
   a. finds some playing cards   **b.** reads to Jim   **c.** hears news of the French Revolution   **d.** finds a coin with a crown on it

3. The king that Huck and Jim talk about most is
   a. Louis the Sixteenth   **b.** Louis the Fourteenth   **c.** Solomon   **d.** George the Third

Drawing Conclusions

4. The character most likely to share Huck's view of the "adventure" aboard the wrecked steamboat would probably be
   a. Huck's father   **b.** Jim   **c.** Tom Sawyer   **d.** Widow Douglas

Appreciating Language

5. When Huck speaks of the *truck* they got from the wreck, he means
   a. a small cart   **b.** the various objects   **c.** gold coins   **d.** fruits and vegetables

Using Logic to Find Deeper Meaning

6. King Solomon's purpose in proposing to chop the child in two was to
   a. give both women an equal share   **b.** discover the true mother   **c.** show how powerful he was   **d.** frighten the child

THINKING IT OVER

Do Jim's arguments that French people should speak English sound logical? How would you go about convincing Jim that it *is* natural for a French person to speak differently from an American?

CHAPTER 12

Remembering Detail

1. When they get to Cairo, Huck and Jim plan to
   a. take a steamboat to New Orleans   b. settle down there
   c. find Tom Sawyer   d. take a steamboat up the Ohio River

2. Huck and Jim become separated because
   a. Jim falls asleep   b. Huck is unable to tie the raft
   securely   c. Huck wants to play a joke on Jim   d. Huck gets
   lost on the riverbank

3. When Huck finds the raft again
   a. Jim is missing   b. Jim thinks Huck is a ghost   c. Jim falls
   asleep   d. Jim is angry that Huck had been gone so long

4. Huck lies to Jim
   a. to protect himself   b. out of kindness   c. as a joke
   d. to avoid an argument

Identifying the Tone

5. When Jim discovers the trick Huck has played on him, he feels
   a. relieved   b. angry and hurt   c. amused   d. grateful

6. After he has played the trick, Huck feels
   a. proud   b. happy   c. ashamed   d. amused

Using Logic to Find Deeper Meaning

7. When Huck talks about *humbling* himself, he means
   a. apologizing to Jim   b. cheering Jim up   c. doing something
   kind for Jim   d. cleaning up the raft

THINKING IT OVER

Do you think that Huck thought much about Jim's feelings before
he played the trick on him? Explain.

CHAPTER 13

Finding the Main Idea

1. The purpose of this chapter is to show how
   a. much people dread smallpox **b.** Huck and Jim become separated **c.** kindhearted the men in the boat are **d.** Huck and Jim discover they have passed Cairo

Remembering Detail

2. Huck's conscience tells him that
   a. slavery is wrong **b.** he should be kinder to Jim **c.** he was wrong to help Jim escape **d.** it is wrong to lie

3. Huck is shocked that Jim
   a. would steal his children away from their owner **b.** wants to get to Cairo **c.** doesn't trust him **d.** wants to be free

4. Huck keeps the men in the boat from boarding the raft by
   a. telling them his father has chills **b.** making them think that someone on the raft has smallpox **c.** telling them the person on the raft is white **d.** telling them that Jim has yellow fever

5. Huck and Jim know they have passed Cairo when
   a. they see high ground on the shore **b.** they cross the Kentucky state line **c.** they see clear water near the shore and muddy water outside **d.** they meet the steamboat

Identifying the Tone

6. Which of the following best describes Huck's feelings after he lies to the men about smallpox?
   a. happy **b.** mixed **c.** ashamed **d.** proud

Drawing Conclusions

7. The two men in the boat give Huck money because
   a. they know he needs it for a steamboat ticket **b.** they feel guilty about not helping a boy with a sick father **c.** they expect to be paid back **d.** they believe that money will ward off smallpox

8. Huck and Jim continue down the river after missing Cairo because
   a. Jim no longer wants to go North to the free states **b.** Huck doesn't want Jim to be free **c.** the raft cannot go upstream **d.** they want to find their lost canoe

Using Logic to Find Deeper Meaning

9. The two men tell Huck to float twenty miles before trying to go ashore because
   a. they don't want anyone with smallpox nearer than that **b.** better medical care is available there **c.** people down the river aren't afraid of smallpox **d.** it will be easier getting the raft to shore downstream

THINKING IT OVER

Huck's conscience bothers him for helping Jim get away from "his rightful owner." He is also shocked at Jim's plan to free his children, by stealing them if necessary. How does Huck's attitude toward slavery compare with our attitude today? Explain.

CHAPTER 14

Finding the Main Idea

1. The chapter is mostly about
   a. feuding **b.** how the Grangerfords take Huck in **c.** Huck's search for Jim **d.** the story Huck makes up about his family

Remembering Details

2. The Grangerfords were cautious about letting Huck in the house because they
   a. feared all strangers **b.** didn't want to catch smallpox **c.** thought he might be a Shepherdson **d.** were on the lookout for robbers

3. Buck and Huck are about
   a. nine or ten years old **b.** thirteen or fourteen years old **c.** sixteen years old **d.** seventeen or eighteen years old

4. When Huck forgets what his name is supposed to be, he learns it by
   a. getting Buck to spell it **b.** asking Mr. Grangerford **c.** asking his servant **d.** waiting to see what people call him

5. The number of slaves owned by the Grangerfords was about
   a. fifty **b.** a dozen **c.** a hundred **d.** five hundred

Drawing Conclusions

6. Buck is happy to see Huck because
   a. he will have someone to help him with his chores   **b.** he is eager to hear about Huck's travels   **c.** he wants to hear news about Tom Sawyer   **d.** he is glad to have a new friend

Identifying the Tone

7. Which of the following best describes Huck's feelings about the Grangerford family and their house?
   a. impressed   **b.** unimpressed   **c.** resentful   **d.** envious

Appreciating Language

8. When Buck tells Huck they can have *booming times,* he means
   a. noisy times   **b.** good times   **c.** target practice   **d.** easy living

Using Logic to Find Deeper Meaning

9. The story Huck makes up about his family is full of death and disaster because
   a. Huck would rather lie than tell the truth   **b.** he wants the Grangerfords to feel sorry for him   **c.** those things really happened   **d.** he wants to convince them that he is not a Shepherdson

THINKING IT OVER

What does the description of the Grangerfords and their house tell you about the kind of life they lead? Explain your answer.

CHAPTER 15

Remembering Detail

1. The feud between the families began over
   a. a dispute about land   **b.** an elopement   **c.** a runaway slave   **d.** an insult

2. While Huck has been living with the Grangerfords, Jim has been living
   a. on the raft   **b.** in the slave quarters   **c.** with the Shepherdsons   **d.** in a nearby swamp

3. After the collision with the steamboat, Jim does not answer Huck's calls because
   a. he is injured   **b.** he has water in his lungs   **c.** he is afraid of being captured   **d.** he wants to surprise Huck

4. Huck feels partly to blame for the final fight between the families because he
   a. has kept the note to Sophia a secret   **b.** was present when Buck shot at Harney Shepherdson   **c.** overslept   **d.** knew about the feud

Drawing Conclusions

5. When Sophia hears that Buck has shot at Harney, she turns pale because she
   a. hates violence   **b.** is in love with Harney   **c.** is afraid of guns   **d.** is worried about Buck

6. Harney does not shoot Buck when he has the chance because
   a. Buck is Sophia's brother   **b.** Harney is cowardly   **c.** he doesn't want to hit Huck by mistake   **d.** Buck is too young for him to bother with

Identifying the Tone

7. Which of the following best describes Huck's feelings at the end of the fight between the feuding families?
   a. excited   **b.** disgusted   **c.** afraid   **d.** sad

Using Logic to Find Deeper Meaning

8. It is clear that neither the Grangerfords nor the Shepherdsons take the sermon on brotherly love to heart since
   a. they do not shake hands after church **b.** the men bring guns to church **c.** Harney and Sophia elope **d.** the families have a bloody battle the next day

THINKING IT THROUGH

The Grangerfords and the Shepherdsons are both wealthy and civilized families. Yet they behave in a cruel and inhuman way when they feud. How would you explain the contrast between their civilized way of life and their savage behavior toward each other?

CHAPTER 16

Finding the Main Idea

1. The chapter is mostly about
   a. how Huck escapes from the Shepherdsons **b.** the king and the duke **c.** life on the raft **d.** Huck's and Jim's future plans

Remembering Detail

2. When they board the raft, the king and the duke
   a. have known each other for a long time **b.** pretend to be father and son **c.** don't know each other **d.** are hunting for escaped slaves

3. The duke claims that he is really
   a. King Louis the Seventeenth **b.** the rightful Duke of Bridgewater **c.** King George the Third **d.** a secret agent

4. The king claims that he is
   a. the lost Dauphin of France **b.** a duke **c.** Napoleon's son **d.** Charlemagne

5. The duke's plan to make traveling by day safe involves
   a. abandoning Jim **b.** keeping Jim out of sight **c.** keeping rifles on the raft **d.** pretending they are returning Jim to his owner downriver

Drawing Conclusions

6. When the king tells fortunes, he needs someone to find out facts so that he

   a. can pretend to learn these facts from the cards   **b.** can learn whether his predictions come true   **c.** won't tell the fortune of anyone who might get angry   **d.** won't waste time on people who can't pay

Identifying the Tone

7. When Huck and Jim set off on the raft again, they feel

   a. lonesome   **b.** contented   **c.** frightened   **d.** discouraged

Using Logic to Find Deeper Meaning

8. The king and the duke agree that a runaway slave would not run south because

   a. the climate is too hot   **b.** the South is all slave states, where a runaway would have little chance of remaining free
   c. a black man would be highly noticeable in the South
   d. Huck says so

THINKING IT OVER

Huck has been careful all along to keep Jim's presence on the raft a secret, yet he takes the duke and the king right to their hiding place. How would you explain this action of Huck's?

CHAPTER 17

Finding the Main Idea
1. This chapter is mostly about
   a. a feud   b. the shooting of Boggs   c. Colonel Sherburn's war record   d. a performance of *Romeo and Juliet*

Remembering Detail
2. The person who seems to know most about putting on *Romeo and Juliet* is
   a. Colonel Sherburn   b. the duke   c. the king   d. Huck
3. The town is crowded the day of the play because
   a. a circus is in town   b. the steamboat has just landed
   c. it is harvest time   d. people have come to see the fight between Boggs and Colonel Sherburn
4. The price for an adult to see the play is
   a. $1   b. 10¢   c. 25¢   d. $2

Drawing Conclusions
5. Circus day is a good time to put on a play because
   a. it is a holiday   b. country people come to town for the circus   c. the circus is not very good   d. it is Colonel Sherburn's birthday

Identifying the Tone
6. You can tell from the chapter that Boggs is a
   a. dangerous fellow   b. man who threatens but is really harmless   c. highly respected member of the community   d. criminal wanted by the police

Appreciating Language
7. When Colonel Sherburn says the mob lacks *pluck,* he means that the people in it lack
   a. courage   b. money   c. imagination   d. energy

THINKING IT OVER
When the mob disbands, Huck goes along with the others. Does this action show him to be as cowardly as Colonel Sherburn says the mob is? Explain your answer.

CHAPTER 18

Finding the Main Idea
1. This chapter is mostly about
   a. the lynching of Colonel Sherburn   **b.** *Romeo and Juliet*
   c. the new show put on by the duke and the king   **d.** life in
   Arkansas

Remembering Detail
2. Huck sneaks into the circus tent because
   a. he has no money for a ticket   **b.** he doesn't want to waste
   his money   **c.** Jim needs money for a ticket   **d.** the duke tells
   him not to pay for a ticket
3. The number of people who come to see *Romeo and Juliet* is
   a. 12   **b.** two   **c.** more than 100   **d.** none
4. Tickets for the second show cost
   a. less than tickets for *Romeo and Juliet*   **b.** the same as for
   Romeo and Juliet   **c.** twice as much as for *Romeo and
   Juliet*   **d.** whatever people want to contribute
5. The amount the duke and the king take in from their show is
   a. $20   **b.** $8   **c.** $320   **d.** $465

Drawing Conclusions
6. The drunk man at the circus who wants to ride is really
   a. a circus stunt rider   **b.** Huck's father   **c.** Colonel
   Sherburn   **d.** the duke in disguise

Identifying the Tone
7. Which of the following best describes Huck's reaction to the
   circus?
   a. bored   **b.** delighted   **c.** envious   **d.** angry

Appreciating Language
8. When Huck says the circus was *bully,* he means that it was
   a. filled with animals   **b.** coarse   **c.** terrible   **d.** excellent

THINKING IT OVER
How do the people of the town plan to revenge themselves on the
duke and the king? How do the king and the duke outwit them?
Explain.

CHAPTER 19

Finding the Main Idea

1. This chapter is mostly about how
   a. the king leads a prayer meeting **b.** the king and the duke try to trick the Wilks family **c.** Huck meets Mary Jane **d.** Mary Jane exposes the duke

Remembering Detail

2. Jim is kept tied up on the raft all day so that he
   a. will look like a captured runaway slave **b.** won't take the raft and leave **c.** won't come into town and get caught **d.** will be sorry he has run away

3. Peter Wilks had two brothers who lived in
   a. England **b.** St. Louis **c.** New Orleans **d.** France

4. In this chapter, the duke pretends to be
   a. the Duke of Bridgewater **b.** a great actor **c.** Peter Wilks's deaf and dumb brother **d.** the lost dauphin

Drawing Conclusions

5. The king doesn't go aboard the steamboat as he had planned because
   a. he had formed the idea of cheating the Wilks family **b.** he no longer wants to go to New Orleans **c.** he is feeling seasick **d.** he is afraid he cannot imitate a preacher successfully

Identifying Tone

6. The word that best describes Huck's feelings about the scheme to trick the Wilks family is
   a. amusement **b.** fear **c.** excitement **d.** shame

THINKING IT OVER

1. Compare the scheme to cheat the Wilks family with the earlier swindles of the duke and the king. Explain how this dishonest act differs from the others.

2. Huck is disgusted and ashamed of the actions of the duke and the king. Why do you suppose he does not tell the townspeople that the duke and the king are frauds? Explain your answer.

CHAPTER 20

Finding the Main Idea
1. This chapter is mostly about how Huck
   a. feels at the funeral **b.** steals and hides the money **c.** prevents the slaves from being sold **d.** writes a letter to Mary Jane

Remembering Detail
2. The king had hidden the bag of money
   a. in his carpetbag **b.** under a loose board **c.** in the straw mattress on his bed **d.** on the raft
3. Huck takes the money and hides it again
   a. under his own mattress **b.** outside the house **c.** in the slave quarters **d.** in Peter's coffin
4. The king refuses to leave until
   a. all the Wilks's property has been sold **b.** Dr. Robinson apologizes **c.** the slave quarters are torn down **d.** Peter is buried
5. Huck keeps the king and duke from thinking he has stolen the money by
   a. swearing on a Bible **b.** blaming the slaves for the theft **c.** blaming Mary Jane for the theft **d.** causing them to quarrel with each other

Identifying the Tone
6. Which of the following words best describes Huck's attitude toward Mary Jane Wilks?
   a. sympathetic **b.** indifferent **c.** unfriendly **d.** mocking

THINKING IT OVER
1. The king breaks up the slave family for only a small amount of money. What does this show about his character?
2. Compare the king and the duke. Which of these rascals seems to be cleverer? Explain.

CHAPTER 21

Finding the Main Idea

1. In this chapter, the author mostly tells about how
   a. the king and duke are discovered to be frauds   **b.** Huck escapes   **c.** Huck tricks Mary Jane   **d.** Huck hides the money

Remembering Detail

2. Huck asks Mary Jane to leave for the day because
   a. she needs a change   **b.** he fears for her life   **c.** he knows she cannot hide her feelings   **d.** he doesn't want her to be in his way

3. To prove that the king and duke are frauds, Huck gives Mary Jane information about
   a. their claims to being nobility   **b.** the performing of *Royal Nonesuch* up the river   **c.** her real uncles   **d.** his own background

4. The newly arrived men who claim to be Peter Wilks's brothers cannot prove their identity because
   a. no one can understand their English accents   **b.** their baggage has been put off the boat in another town   **c.** the king will not allow them to speak   **d.** the doctor drives them away

Drawing Conclusions

5. If Dr. Robinson did not hold Huck's hand tightly, Huck probably would have
   a. run away   **b.** fallen far behind the group   **c.** joined the king and the duke   **d.** been frightened

Identifying the Tone

6. Which word best describes Huck's feelings when Mary Jane says that she will pray for him?
   a. impatient   **b.** indifferent   **c.** moved   **d.** amused

Using Logic to Find Deeper Meaning

7. Huck cannot tell Mary Jane how he happens to be with the king and the duke because
   a. he is ashamed   **b.** he fears she will be disappointed in him
   c. he doesn't dare tell her about Jim   **d.** he fears that they will beat him

THINKING IT THROUGH

Huck says that he tells Mary Jane the truth because "the truth would be better and *safer* than a lie." Do you think that is the real reason he tells her the truth about the two frauds? Explain your answer.

CHAPTER 22

Finding the Main Idea

1. The purpose of this chapter is to
   a. show how the hidden money is found   **b.** show how the attempt to defraud the Wilks family ends   **c.** introduce Levi Bell   **d.** show what Jim has been doing

Remembering Detail

2. Levi Bell tricks the king and the duke into
   a. admitting they are frauds   **b.** giving him a sample of their handwriting   **c.** telling him where the money is hidden   **d.** giving him a deed to the Wilks's property

3. The townspeople want to dig up Wilks's body in order to
   a. find the money   **b.** see who is buried there   **c.** see if the dead man has a tattoo   **d.** find out the cause of his death

4. The duke and the king quarrel when they get back to the raft because
   a. each thinks the other hid the money in the coffin   **b.** the duke has protected Jim from the king's anger   **c.** their scheme has failed   **d.** they have had too much to drink

Identifying the Tone

5. Which of the following best describes Huck's feelings as the coffin is being opened in the graveyard?
   a. excitement   **b.** grief   **c.** fear   **d.** relief

THINKING IT OVER

1. At the end of the chapter, the duke says to the king, "They have all their money back, and all ours too!" Explain what he is referring to.

2. Have the king and the duke gained anything from their attempt to pose as Peter Wilks's brothers? Consider the sale of the slaves and the auctioning of the house and property as you answer.

CHAPTER 23

Finding the Main Idea

1. This chapter is mostly about
   a. some new moneymaking scheme the king and duke think up   **b.** the king and duke turning Jim in for reward money   **c.** another performance of the *Royal Nonesuch*   **d.** Huck's deciding to travel alone

Remembering Detail

2. One sign that the raft has traveled quite far south is that
   a. the current is stronger   **b.** palm trees grow along the bank   **c.** Spanish moss grows on the trees   **d.** it crosses the Mason-Dixon line

3. For turning Jim in, the king gets
   a. $200   **b.** $800   **c.** nothing   **d.** $40

4. To prove that Jim is a runaway slave, the king uses
   a. the fake handbill the duke printed   **b.** a letter from Miss Watson   **c.** Jim's own confession   **d.** a clipping from a St. Louis paper

5. Huck thinks of writing to Tom Sawyer to tell him
   a. to let Miss Watson know where Jim is   **b.** about his adventures   **c.** to send money to buy Jim's freedom   **d.** how sorry he is to see Jim captured

Drawing Conclusions

6. The secret plan the duke and the king make on the raft is to
   a. sell the raft   **b.** put on another performance of the *Royal Nonesuch*   **c.** turn Jim in for reward money   **d.** rob a house

7. The king is willing to sell his chance at the reward money for far less than the amount offered because
   a. the handbill is a fake   **b.** he doesn't want to wait for the money to be sent up the river   **c.** he feels bad about turning Jim in   **d.** he is afraid Huck will tell people he and the duke are frauds

Appreciating Language

8. When the duke says the handbill offering a reward for Jim is *bogus*, he means that it is
   a. genuine   **b.** fake   **c.** valuable   **d.** official

THINKING IT OVER

1. Huck has strongly conflicting feelings when he finds that Jim has been captured. Explain in your own words both what Huck thinks is right and what he decides to do.

2. In your opinion, is Huck right to disregard what his conscience tells him as far as Jim is concerned?

CHAPTER 24

Finding the Main Idea

1. This chapter is mostly about how Huck
    a. escapes from the duke **b.** is mistaken for Tom Sawyer
    c. finds where Jim is being held **d.** plans to free Jim

Remembering Detail

2. The Phelps's place is a
    a. huge plantation **b.** busy saw mill **c.** general store
    d. small cotton plantation

3. Mrs. Phelps is
    a. Mary Jane Wilks's aunt **b.** Huck's aunt **c.** Tom Sawyer's aunt **d.** Miss Watson's sister

4. Besides being a farmer, Mr. Phelps is a
    a. preacher **b.** sheriff **c.** slave dealer **d.** lawyer

Drawing Conclusions

5. Tom Sawyer is amazed to see Huck because
    a. Tom thinks Huck is back in St. Petersburg **b.** Tom thinks Huck has been murdered **c.** Huck has changed so much **d.** Huck is wearing Tom's clothing

6. When he says Mr. Phelps "never charged anything for his preaching, and it was worth it, too," Huck is suggesting that
    a. Mr. Phelps was generous **b.** Mr. Phelps was a great preacher **c.** Mr. Phelps was not much of a preacher
    d. Mr. Phelps never preached

THINKING IT OVER

When Tom Sawyer agrees to help Huck steal Jim, Huck says, "Tom Sawyer fell quite a bit, in my opinion of him." Explain why Huck should be surprised at Tom's doing what he wants to do himself.

CHAPTER 25

Remembering Detail

1. Tom convinces Mr. and Mrs. Phelps that he is
   a. an orphan **b.** his brother Sid **c.** Huck Finn
   d. Harvey Wilks

2. The person who reveals to the people of Pikeville that the duke and the king are frauds is
   a. Huck **b.** Dr. Robinson **c.** Jim **d.** Mr. Phelps

3. To punish the duke and the king, the townspeople
   a. hang them **b.** tar and feather them **c.** put them in jail **d.** drown them

4. Tom and Huck learn that Jim is being kept in
   a. a cabin behind the Phelps's house **b.** the town jail
   c. the schoolhouse **d.** a cage

Drawing Conclusions

5. Tom reasons that the plate of food being taken to the cabin is intended for a man because
   a. he already knows someone is in the cabin **b.** people don't feed animals watermelon **c.** the cabin is locked **d.** the Phelps have too many dogs to feed with one plate of food

6. Huck can pretend to be Tom, and Tom can pretend to be his brother Sid because
   a. neither Aunt Sally nor her husband can see well **b.** Tom and Sid are twins **c.** Huck and Tom look a lot alike **d.** the Phelpses have never seen either Tom or Sid

THINKING IT OVER

1. Do you think Huck's plan for freeing Jim would have worked? Explain your reasoning.

2. Tom rejects Huck's plan as being too simple. What kind of a plan do you suppose Tom has thought of? Where would he be likely to get his ideas for a rescue?

CHAPTER 26

Finding the Main Idea

1. This chapter is mostly about
   a. putting Tom's rescue plan into operation   **b.** superstitions
   c. frightening Aunt Sally   **d.** Huck's reunion with Jim

Remembering Detail

2. Nat ties tufts of his hair with thread to
   a. keep it from blowing   **b.** keep it clean   **c.** ward off
   witches   **d.** make it look better

3. When Tom's Uncle Silas learns that Jim has not run away from
   New Orleans, he will probably
   a. let Jim go free   **b.** advertise Jim   **c.** have Jim put in jail
   d. hand Jim over to a slave dealer

4. Tom and Huck leave their room at night by means of
   a. a secret passage   **b.** a rope ladder   **c.** a lightning rod
   d. the backstairs

5. What does Aunt Sally give Huck and Tom for letting snakes
   loose in her house?
   a. a scolding   **b.** a licking   **c.** a warning   **d.** a big hug

Drawing Conclusions

6. Tom's ideas about prison life and escapes from prison probably
   come from
   a. his experience   **b.** school books   **c.** adventure stories
   d. newspapers

7. Tom insists on bringing rats to Jim's cabin because
   a. he thinks Jim needs company   **b.** the prisoners he has read
   about all have to deal with rats   **c.** they will gnaw a hole in
   the cabin   **d.** he wants to punish Jim for running away

THINKING IT OVER

Tom resists Huck's practical ideas, such as digging with picks instead
of knives and using a real saw instead of making one from a knife
blade. Explain why Tom never wants to do things the easy way.

CHAPTER 27

Remembering Detail

1. Uncle Silas never gets a reply to his letters to the plantation listed on the handbill because
   a. the owner can not write   **b.** there is no such plantation
   c. the owner doesn't want to pay the reward   **d.** the duke had written the address wrong

2. Aunt Sally catches Huck
   a. writing an anonymous letter   **b.** letting a garter snake loose   **c.** taking butter from the cellar   **d.** sliding down the lightning rod

3. Huck quickly hides the butter
   a. on the cellar steps   **b.** in his hat   **c.** in his pocket
   d. on a windowsill

4. The dogs don't attack Huck, Tom, and Jim because
   a. the dogs recognize them   **b.** the dogs don't see them
   c. Huck gives them chunks of meat   **d.** the three are already in the canoe

Drawing Conclusions

5. Tom decides to write the anonymous letters in order to
   a. make the rescue safer   **b.** stir up more excitement   **c.** scare Aunt Sally   **d.** put off the rescue attempt

Identifying the Tone

6. Which of the following best describes Huck's feelings when he hears that Uncle Silas is going to advertise Jim in the St. Louis papers?
   a. anger   **b.** relief   **c.** fright   **d.** sorrow

THINKING IT OVER

Huck says that Tom is "gladdest of all" because he has a bullet in his leg. Taking into account what you know about Tom, explain why he would be glad to be wounded.

CHAPTER 28

Remembering Detail

1. To explain Tom's wound, Huck tells the doctor that Tom had
   a. been shot helping a slave escape   **b.** been shot by outlaws
   c. shot himself in his sleep   **d.** been shot while cleaning his gun

2. Huck stays with the Phelpses instead of returning to the raft because
   a. he is afraid he will be followed   **b.** Aunt Sally begs him not to leave   **c.** the doctor has not returned the canoe   **d.** he is too tired

3. Aunt Sally does not read the letter she has just received because
   a. the wounded Tom is brought home just then   **b.** she recognizes Jim   **c.** she is angry with Aunt Polly   **d.** she misplaces it

4. The men want to hang Jim
   a. as a warning to other slaves who might run away   **b.** because they couldn't lynch Colonel Sherburn   **c.** because he is blamed for Tom's injury   **d.** because he wrote the anonymous letters

Drawing Conclusions

5. When Huck tells the doctor how Tom was shot, the doctor probably
   a. believes Huck's story   **b.** knows Huck is lying   **c.** doesn't want to be involved in any trouble   **d.** knows that Tom has helped a runaway slave

6. The men do not hang Jim because
   a. it would be a crime to kill a slave for running away
   b. Huck begs them not to   **c.** they are afraid they would have to pay Jim's owner for him   **d.** they sympathize with his desire to be free

THINKING IT OVER

The doctor tells the men that Jim has risked his freedom to care for Tom. He adds, a person "like that is worth kind treatment." In view of the other things you now know about Jim's character, are you surprised that he acts as he does? Explain your answer.

CHAPTER 29

Finding the Main Idea

1. The main purpose of this chapter is
   a. to reveal that Pap is dead **b.** to tie up all loose ends of the plot **c.** to introduce Aunt Polly **d.** to tell that Huck will be living with the Phelpses from now on

Remembering Detail

2. Aunt Sally learns who wrote the anonymous letters from
   a. Uncle Silas **b.** the doctor **c.** Tom **d.** Huck

3. Aunt Polly comes to visit her sister because she
   a. needs a vacation **b.** hears that Tom and Sid are visiting Aunt Sally **c.** wants to claim part of the Wilks's inheritance
   d. believes that Huck Finn is alive

4. Huck learns that Pap is dead from
   a. Aunt Polly **b.** Tom Sawyer **c.** Judge Thatcher **d.** Jim

5. The person who gives Jim his freedom is
   a. Huck **b.** Tom Sawyer **c.** Miss Watson **d.** Uncle Silas

THINKING IT OVER

1. Tom Sawyer cooks up a dangerous plan to free Jim, knowing all the time that Jim is already a free man. Why does he do this? In your opinion, was this a good thing to do? Give your reasons.

2. At the end of the book, Huck says he can't stand the thought of being adopted and "civilized" by Aunt Sally. What aspects of life with the Phelpses would Huck find hard to bear, particularly after Tom goes back to Missouri?